seasons of
LINCOLN

Cover image by Joel Sartore

Photography on the following pages, as well as in chapters one through four by Joel Sartore:

14, 16, 17, 84, 86, 92, 140

Corporate profile photography in chapters five through nine by John F. Sanders

Contributing photography on the following pages by Pat McDonogh:

8, 12, 13, 15, 18, 36 (top right and bottom left), 52, 53 (top), 56 (bottom), 57, 60, 103, 104, 119, 120

Library of Congress Cataloging-in Publication-Data

Burchfield, Gary F.
    Seasons of Lincoln : written by Gary Burchfield; featuring
    the photography of Joel Sartore; contributing photography
    by Pat McDonogh; corporate profile photography by
    John Sanders.—1st ed.
        p. cm.
    Includes bibliographical references and index.
    ISBN 1-58192-040-7
    1. Lincoln (Neb.)—Economic conditions. 2. Lincoln (Neb.)—
Social conditions. 3. Lincoln (Neb.)—Description and travel.
I. Title.
HC108.L43B87 2001
330.9782'293—dc21   2001003820

seasons of
LINCOLN

WRITTEN BY GARY BURCHFIELD
CORPORATE PROFILES BY GARY BURCHFIELD
FEATURING THE PHOTOGRAPHY OF JOEL SARTORE
CONTRIBUTING PHOTOGRAPHY BY PAT MCDONOGH
CORPORATE PROFILE PHOTOGRAPHY BY JOHN F. SANDERS

seasons of

LINCOLN

Written by Gary Burchfield
Corporate profiles by Gary Burchfield
Featuring the photography of Joel Sartore
Contributing photography by Pat McDonogh
Corporate profile photography by John F. Sanders

Community Communications, Inc.
Publisher: Ronald P. Beers

Staff for *Seasons of Lincoln*
Acquisitions: Ronald P. Beers
Publisher's Sales Associate: Rickey Heaton
Editor In Chief: Wendi L. Lewis
Managing Editor: Christi Stevens
Profile Editor: Mary Catherine Richardson
Editorial Assistants: Debra C. Carroll and
Krewe Maynard
Proofreader: Heather Ann Edwards
Design Director: Scott Phillips
Designer: Matt Johnson
Photo Editors: Christi Stevens and
Matt Johnson
National Sales Manager: Keely Smith
Sales Assistants: Annette Lozier and
Brandon Maddox
Accounting Services: Stephanie Perez
Print Production Manager: Jarrod Stiff
Pre-Press and Separations:
Artcraft Graphic Productions

CCI

Community Communications, Inc.
Montgomery, Alabama

David M. Williamson, *Chief Executive Officer*
Ronald P. Beers, *President*
W. David Brown, *Chief Operating Officer*

©2001 Community Communications, Inc.
All Rights Reserved
Published 2001
Printed in USA
First Edition

Library of Congress Cataloging Number:
2001003820
ISBN Number: 1-58192-040-7

Every effort has been made to ensure
the accuracy of the information herein.
However, the authors and Community
Communications are not responsible for any
errors or omissions that might have occurred.

Table of Contents

PART ONE

PART TWO

Seasons of Change

Sometimes, driving through Lincoln, I try to imagine what the area must have looked like to the early pioneers and settlers. Coming up a narrow, winding trail from the east and topping a rise, endless miles of tall grass prairie roll away to the west. The treeless horizon is so distant it almost seems to blend with the blue sky.

Closer, the terrain slopes gently downward toward a basin where small ponds of water glint in the bright sun. Along the edges of the ponds, a whitish rime reflects the mid-day sun—salt! The white gold of medieval times. Other trails lead into the basin from several directions.

Moving down the slope, the waving grass brushes the stirrups. A startled antelope and her fawn bound away. Off to the right, a little swale holds a small spring oozing water and a couple of scrub trees. The Native tribes that visit the basin call the little swale "Wyuka," or "place where he rests."

Farther on, a meandering stream bank begins to take shape. Along its edges, unusual plants, salt-loving forbs and reeds meld with the tall grass.

My own first visit to Lincoln was much less auspicious. I arrived on a Greyhound bus in June, 1952, McGrew High School's representative to Cornhusker Boys' State. My folks were too busy with ranch work to drive me to Lincoln. Besides, there was no Interstate-80 those days, just venerable old Highway 30 that wound through about every town along the Platte River.

I was intimidated by the big city, but soon was safely ensconced at University of Nebraska at Lincoln with about three hundred other boys. I think we were bunked in somewhere on East Campus. I do remember one of my counselors for the week was Bobby Reynolds. What a big deal it was to see this superhero in person.

A year later, I was back, this time as a University of Nebraska freshman—red beanie and all! Four memorable years went by all too fast, and then I was off to make my way, first as a young Marine second lieutenant, then on to civilian pursuits, none of which were nearly as exciting as the Marine Corps. By 1971, I was ready to leave an advertising job in California and return to…Lincoln!

I guess, after thirty years now, I qualify as a native, though I'm sure there are some "real natives" who might argue the point with me. Nevertheless, it has been my good fortune to witness Lincoln's amazing growth. Yes, I'll admit, I sometimes grumble about the traffic on O Street. Fact is, I try not to be on O Street between 3:30 and 5:30 p.m.

By and large, however, Lincoln is still a small town. It just pretends to be a big city these days! Those of us who have been around awhile marvel at all the apartment complexes, the new business and commercial structures springing up, the luxury homes and all the new eateries with cute names. But it's still a great hometown. Still a place to come back to. Still a place with roots.

Living in one place for thirty years, one can't help but assimilate much of the culture and a lot of the history of the place. Preparing the editorial material for this book has provided a great opportunity to explore even more about Lincoln's past and to track down some of the most interesting "tidbits" about the city.

It also has been my privilege to meet and interview people in some of Lincoln's finest companies and organizations…including many who have "broken the trail" for Lincoln's remarkable growth.

My hope, as you read through the following pages, is that you, too, will discover some new things about this very special place on the plains that we call home.

Gary Burchfield

part

ONE

BryanLGH Medical Center

BryanLGH is a 583-bed, not-for-profit, locally owned healthcare organization with two acute-care facilities and many outpatient clinics. Premiere specialties include cardiology, trauma, neurology/neurosurgery, mental health, oncology, and orthopedics. The Medical Center is listed as one of the 100 top hospitals in the nation for cardiac and stroke care. BryanLGH spans the state through a network that provides sophisticated mobile diagnostic treatment and services to citizens throughout the region. Through the Heartland Health Alliance, a 32-hospital statewide network, BryanLGH has forged strong partnerships with hospitals, physicians, and communities, to ensure that cost-effective, high-quality health care is available throughout Nebraska.

THE GOODYEAR TIRE & RUBBER COMPANY

Lincoln's Goodyear facilities are key elements in Goodyear's worldwide operations. National marketing headquarters for Replacement Products, Hose, and Power Transmission Products (PTP) are based in Lincoln. Goodyear's worldwide computer information system for Engineered Products is part of Goodyear-Lincoln, as is the company's Global Distribution Center at Lincoln's Airpark West. The Worldwide PTP Technical Center also is part of the Lincoln facilities.

From its first World War II manufacturing operation in Lincoln, Goodyear has expanded its operating facilities to 10 times the original size. Along with being one of Lincoln's largest industrial employers, Goodyear contributes some $120 million annually to the local area economy. Its staff and employees have contributed countless hours and funds to community organizations.

HOME Real Estate

HOME Real Estate represents more than 50 of Lincoln's finest homebuilders and has played a major role in such new home developments as The Highlands, Southern Hills, North Ridge, Country View Estates, Pine Lake Heights, and Wilderness Ridge. HOME Real Estate's role in Lincoln's continuing growth is not surprising, since the company ranks 92nd among the country's 500 largest real estate brokers and 47th among the largest privately owned independent real estate firms. HOME Real Estate serves the Lincoln community from six primary offices. Through association with other firms, HOME offers its clients complete real estate services, including lot sales, new construction sales, in-house lending, and title insurance services.

PFIZER

The largest manufacturing site for Pfizer animal health products is in Lincoln. Pfizer Inc is a global, research-based pharmaceutical company known the world over for a variety of advanced medicines. Veterinarians, livestock producers, and pet owners are probably more familiar with Pfizer's biological and pharmaceutical products for cattle, swine, horses, dogs, and cats.

Pfizer operations in Lincoln today occupy nearly 900,000 square feet of laboratory, office, and manufacturing space and is one of Lincoln's top industrial employers, with more than 800 employees.

Pfizer Lincoln proudly accepted the Mayor's first annual Community Conscience Award in 2000 for its outstanding record as a corporate citizen. The award recognized Pfizer's role in supporting nonprofit organizations and the company's participation in building a healthy Lincoln community.

SAINT ELIZABETH REGIONAL MEDICAL CENTER

Saint Elizabeth has been a leading medical provider since 1889, when four pioneering Sisters of St. Francis of Perpetual Adoration opened Lincoln's first hospital in a home on South Street. Today, Saint Elizabeth is a major economic factor in the community as well as a regional referral medical center.

Saint Elizabeth opened the region's first Burn Center in 1973 and is still the area's primary trauma center for burn patients and also houses a rapidly growing cardiovascular program providing a full range of heart procedures. As Saint Elizabeth Regional Medical Center moves on into the new millennium, it continues to focus on its mission to nurture the healing ministry of the church by bringing it new life, energy, and viability in the 21st century.

WELLS FARGO BANK

Nebraska's first Wells Fargo office opened in 1867, providing express services for the frontier West. Today, Wells Fargo is Nebraska's second largest bank network, with 48 store locations and over 180 ATMs around the state. No longer in the express business, Wells Fargo today is a diversified financial services company providing banking, insurance, investments, mortgage and consumer finance services.

Wells Fargo ranks number one in the industry for small business and agricultural lending, commercial real estate lending, mortgage origination and online financial services. Wells Fargo is the country's second largest SBA lender.

Wells Fargo Center has had a banking presence in downtown Lincoln since 1902. The Wells Fargo Center, constructed in 1976, is a noted Lincoln landmark.

chapter one

SPRING

◧

Washington, DC, may have its cherry blossoms, but Lincoln has its crab apple blossoms. They burst forth in a profusion of dainty white, pink, or reddish flowers as if to trumpet: "Wake up everyone. Spring is here again."

Add to those the blooms of the redbuds, the lilacs, the crocus, the early iris, the daffodils, and naturally, the dandelions that refuse to be left out of the color mix. Yes, it's spring in Lincoln and an eons-old process of rebirth and new growth begins again. It's a magnificent time. The skies are a little bluer; the clouds a little puffier; the bird songs a little louder; and even the evergreens have some new green to show off.

Of course, spring in this part of the country can be somewhat fickle. Some think of spring as "the turbulent season." It can be spring-like one day and snowing the next, or 95 degrees at noon and 45 degrees by dark. Like most Nebraskans, Lincoln residents proudly declare to the newcomer that "if you don't like the weather, wait five minutes and it will change." Sure enough, it usually does!

Spring blizzards can and do surprise us every so often, as one did on April 21, 1992, when green lawns and leafed-out trees were buried under deep drifts of snow. An Easter Sunday blizzard in 1873 reportedly took the lives of many early settlers.

Tornadoes are a spring phenomenon, too. Fortunately, Lincoln has been spared major tornado damage, but twisters have touched down in the outskirts of town and in nearby villages like Garland, Ceresco, Milford, and Palmyra.

Nevertheless, most springtimes in the capital city are just like we ordered them, cooling breezes, warming sun, and gentle rains. It's a time of reawakening, rejuvenation, and anticipation. A time to clean up the tackle box, check the outboard motor, plant the garden, and get after the crabgrass. It's time to head to the Farmers Market on Saturday mornings, the Foundation Gardens Wednesdays at noon, and Antelope Park weekend evenings. In short, it's time to get out and do.

For the ancients, spring was announced by the first thunderstorm of the season. Meteorologists have determined that spring really begins with the vernal equinox, which falls somewhere around March 21. We who call Lincoln home know that spring really begins when the crab apples bloom. ▪

Along with the sensory fragrance of fresh fruits and vegetables, one can find just about every kind of homemade pastry, bread, jam, jelly, or honey. You can even order buffalo steaks to grill at home.

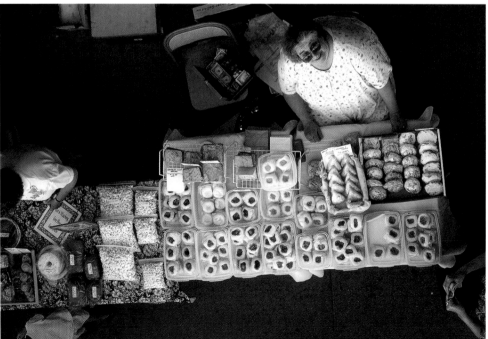

Crafts, entertainment, fresh produce—it's all part of the "festival atmosphere" at Farmers Market. More than 110 vendors open up shop every Saturday morning.

Spring means flowers and every Saturday morning is
Farmers Market time in Lincoln's Haymarket.
It begins in early May and runs through October.

Everybody loves the Farmers Market. You meet all kinds of new friends. The average number of "people" visitors each Saturday approaches 5,000.

"Baby Needs Shoes" is just one of the musical groups that entertain noon-hour audiences on Wednesdays in downtown Lincoln. Foundation Gardens, 15th and N Streets, is the place to be every Wednesday at noon from mid-May through September.

Around Lincoln, there are plenty of venues for spring and summer fun, including the annual Camp Creek Threshers' antique machinery show near Waverly, Bethany in Bloom, Havelock's annual parade and run, Denton Daze, and others. And, there are always special events at State Fair Park, the Lied Center and Pershing Auditorium.
• Gardners look forward to the annual "Spring Affair" at State Fair Park in late April.
• "Haymarket Heydays" brings entertainers, food vendors and revelers to the Haymarket in mid-June.
• The annual "Cornhusker State Games" brings close to 14,000 competitors to Lincoln from throughout the state in mid-July.
• It wouldn't be summer without the annual Shrine Bowl football game in July. The 43rd annual all-star game was held in 2001.
• Lincoln Children's Museum stays open until 8 p.m. Thursdays in July and August for "Dollar Dinner Nights."

Bring your brown bag or pick up treats from the nearby Original Korn Popper and enjoy a variety of performing arts at Lincoln Foundation Gardens.

Local groups, including the Irish Dancers, present free summer concerts every weekend at Antelope Park.

Lincoln is a city of historic homes and spring signals the time to brush away winter's residue and refresh yards and gardens. Mt. Emerald Historic District in the near south neighborhood was Lincoln's first National Historic District in 1980. The south bottoms neighborhood was added to the list in 1986, because of its importance in early immigration of Germans from Russia. Both William Jennings Bryan's "Fairview" and the Nebraska State Capitol are National Historic Landmarks.

Although a city on the move, Lincoln is a community of heritage, as well as tradition.

Homeowners have banded together to maintain and improve Lincoln neighborhoods, along with restoring many of the city's historic homes.

Lincoln has a rich history of buildings, both homes and commercial structures. The city now includes three National Register of Historic Places areas and ten Local Landmark District designations, plus more than 50 individual properties not included in either designation.

The first floor of Historic Eastlake Manor, built by the Yates family in Queen Anne style, can be reserved for wedding receptions and other events.

Historic Eastlake Manor, originally built in 1890, is being restored by members of the Brandt family, which purchased the home in 1937. Nine original stained glass windows are still in place. The home is open for tours by special arrangement, and even has it's own Web site, www.historiceastlake.com.

Once covered with thick tall-grass prairie, Lancaster County still provides lush grazing for more than 30,000 bovine residents.

Long before pioneers moved into the Salt Creek basin, bison and other wildlife frequented the many salt licks in the area. You can still see bison at Pioneers Park.

The unique environment of the Salt Creek basin provides habitat

for such rare specimens as the Salt Creek Tiger Beetle.

Entomologists seek more information on Salt Creek Tiger Beetle populations, as well as other inhabitants of the Salt Creek streambed.

Many people do not realize that Folsom Children's Zoo is also a botanical garden with more than 400 plant species, including 50 different types of trees.

Folsom Children's Zoo is an educational treat for all and especially fun for kids at the Critter Encounter Area, where they can pet the goats, ride the turtle, and get face to face with other friendly critters.

One-third of the animals at the Children's Zoo are on threatened or endangered species lists, such as the African Dwarf Crocodile.

*More than 300 animals
and birds representing
95 species can be seen
and enjoyed at Folsom
Children's Zoo.*

*The Butterfly Pavilion
at Folsom Children's
Zoo is a 20' x 60'
free-flight aviary where
visitors can walk through
and observe dozens of
butterfly species.*

*Many Lincoln
neighborhoods and
community groups,
as well as most
churches, host special
Easter programs.*

In 1872, citizens were reporting "deer and coyotes within the city limits of Lincoln." Most of the wildlife today is smaller, and probably more prevalent!

Lincoln is a sports town. From T-ball on up, kids get involved and compete at every grade level.

Some 84 softball divisions play in Lincoln Parks & Recreation programs each summer. Each division includes anywhere from 8 to 15 teams. Lincoln has close to 40 ball fields available for residents. There are leagues for about every age group and skill level.

High school baseball is highly competitive and Lincoln teams typically fare well in state competition. A number of players go on to play at the college level. Now, with the success of the Cornhuskers and the new semi-pro Lincoln Saltdogs, baseball has become a major spectator sport in the capital city.

Downtown Lincoln has become more "interconnected" with skywalks between several office buildings and hotels.

Lincoln's usually plentiful rainfall and summer temperatures foster a wide range of vegetation.

Many neighborhood parks throughout the city are maintained and cared for by volunteers, usually residents of the neighborhood.

University of Nebraska at Lincoln (UNL) alumnus Ralph Mueller gave $85,000 for construction of the bell tower on campus, which was dedicated in 1949. Music is played daily from a computerized keyboard in the tower base.

Several area statues, as well as Sunken Gardens, were created as Works Project Administration (WPA) projects during the Great Depression of the 1930s.

Once a city refuse site, the beautifully terraced Sunken Gardens at 27th and Capitol Parkway provides a perfect setting for summer weddings.

chapter two

SUMMER

◆

Surprisingly, summer is Nebraska's least turbulent season. Wind speeds are slower than any other season—something like 40 percent slower than in January. That's not to say there aren't exceptions. A severe windstorm July 8, 1993, swept across Nebraska downing hundreds of trees. Winds were clocked at 73 mph in Lincoln, leaving many businesses and thousands of homes without power.

Still, summer tornadoes are less frequent than in spring and, interestingly, usually smaller, slower, and weaker. Summer thunderstorms move slower, too, but tend to produce heavier rains and more hail. In July, 1993, volunteers piled sandbags at the entrance to Bob Devaney Sports Center when Antelope Creek threatened to flood. Heavy rains July 6 and 7, 1908, left railroad cars stranded in the Burlington Yards and sent flood waters down Salt Creek to Ashland, which suffered heavy damage.

Lincoln's average high temperature in July is 89.5 degrees, although it did hit 108 degrees in July, 1990, and a blistering 115 degrees on July 25, 1936. Lincoln has sunny days 63 percent of the time, and at least 163 days are safe from frost. And July and August are the only two months when it has never snowed in Lincoln.

Like Lincoln's other seasons, summer can be one of extremes. Most of us have only read about the dust storms of the 1930s, but some of Lincoln's worst dust storms occurred during a 1950 drought. The years 1988 and 1989 also were extremely dry, as was the summer and fall of 2000. Generally, though, Lincoln can expect 26.9 inches of rain every year. August, 1982, saw 8.57 inches in one month!

The weather doesn't stop Lincoln from celebrating, though. Things get underway in June with free jazz concerts Tuesday evenings at the Sheldon Memorial Art Gallery Sculpture Garden. Then it's July 4 in all its civic glory with an all-day celebration at Holmes Lake and the traditional fireworks display. Later in July, Lincoln's July Jamm takes over downtown for three days and nights, featuring music by blues and rock artists.

August kicks off with the fun and friendly competition of the Lancaster County Fair, now at the new Lancaster Events Center, followed a few days later by Ribfest, another downtown celebration with music and outstanding barbecue cooked up by vendors from several states.

All in all, summer in Lincoln is as much like an old fashioned summer as you can find just about anywhere. The weather may get a little sticky sometimes, but by and large, it is a time to have fun and enjoy life. ■

There are 20 public lakes within 25 miles of Lincoln, plus many private farm ponds like this one in Lancaster County.

Antelope Creek Dam was created as a flood control project in 1961. The lake was named Holmes Lake, after George W. Holmes, in 1962. Holmes Lake and the surrounding park area has become summer's playground for kids of all ages.

Hundreds of migrating waterfowl pass through the area, using the city's lakes as brief rest areas—sometimes deciding it's a great place to take up long-term residence.

For the avid fishermen,
summer doesn't get any
better than this!

Nebraska Game & Parks Commission has instituted an
Urban Fisheries Program that includes stocking catchable-size
fish in city ponds, including Lincoln's Oak Lake.

Fishing teaches many things, such as patience, skill, safety, and appreciation for the outdoors.

Despite the capital city's growth, most of Lancaster County's 865 square miles is still rural.

Lincolnites take pride in their homes and landscapes. For good reason—the shade and cooling effects of trees and lawns saves millions of dollars each year in air conditioning and cooling costs.

Lincoln's remarkable growth rate has generated a building boom.

The number of new homes built has averaged 1,017 per year since 1998.

Lincoln is a city of homeowners, with 68 percent of homes occupied by their owners. Average selling price for homes continues to climb. It's now over $122,000.

Newcomers are surprised to learn that one of every four Nebraskans depends on agriculture for employment.

Area farmers often work at jobs in Lincoln during the week and spend their weekends doing farm work.

Despite the spread of city neighborhoods, 96 percent of Nebraska's land area is still devoted to farms and ranches.

Fields surrounding the city grow corn for grain, as well as hybrid seed corn. Many a teenager has spent a summer detasseling seed corn.

The southern portion of Lancaster County, including the Yankee Hill area of Lincoln, was once part of Clay County. Clay County was split in 1864, with the northern 12 miles added to Lancaster County and the southern 12 miles to Gage County.

Busy city folks appreciate the fact that a few minutes travel gets them into the rolling countryside surrounding the capital city.

Lancaster County has more than 421,000 acres in farms, about 82 percent of which are devoted to crops such as corn, soybeans, and milo.

Lincoln's largest park,
Wilderness Park, covers
more than 1,475 acres,
with hiking and biking
trails that stretch over
22 miles round-trip.

Lincoln soon will have six high schools, 36 elementary schools, and 10 middle schools. In addition, more than 8,000 students attend private and parochial schools in the city.

Classes first opened at Lincoln High School in 1915, the only original high school in the city still in use.

Lincoln's school system consistently ranks high in national achievement tests and graduates typically do well in college—level studies.

Lincoln summers are a good time for relaxing.
The average high temperature in July is 89.5 degrees.

A summer day of three-on-three basketball helps keep the shooting eye sharp.

"Dibs on the swing."

Lincoln neighborhoods typically are as friendly as you'll find anywhere. Summer aromas can be tantalizing.

chapter three

AUTUMN

Autumn is called the season of change. That's much too mild a term for the hardy souls that call Lincoln and Nebraska home. Fall in this part of the world is a great deal more than just a change of seasons. It's the time to break out red shirts, red jackets, red caps, and red coveralls. It's the time to slip that favorite shotgun out of the closet and stock up on extra shells. Time to give "Old Bess" a few more dog biscuits for extra energy.

Sure, fall is chore time, too. Clean up garden residue; put on that last lawn fertilization; clip the withered flowers; and rake the leaves. But for most of us, even chore lists get scheduled around Big Red football broadcasts, opening day of pheasant season or deer season, and maybe that last outing to Branched Oak or Pawnee Lake.

We hate to see summer go, but we anticipate the excitement of fall. Already in late August it's time for the Nebraska State Fair and all the entertainment and activity that brings. Shortly, local orchards and berry farms will be offering their tasty delights on-site, whether you purchase or pick 'em yourself.

Yes, the nights begin a little sooner; the shadows get a little longer; and cornfields turn from green to gold almost before you realize it. The bright colors of the milo fields seem to challenge the tree leaves to see which develops the richest colors. The harvest moon looms larger, as if trying to see everything that's going on "down here."

High school football games mean a sweater or jacket. Popcorn becomes more popular than ice cream. And thousands of pumpkins miraculously become jack-o-lanterns, just in time for Halloween.

That special time when "the frost is on the pumpkin and the fodder is in the shock" is suddenly upon us. We look to see if the squirrels have especially fluffy tails to indicate how severe our winter might be. We hear the itinerant honking of geese as they pass overhead on their way south. We enjoy the warm days and get ready for the cold days to follow. ■

Fall is a unique time in "four seasons" climates like Lincoln.
It's a time of transition, a time for reflection . . .
time to make sure the snowblower will start.

Displays like this are designed to capture the attention of moms, dads, and grandparents. It's not pumpkins they see, but jack-o-lanterns, roasted seeds, and treats for tots.

Shorter days mean
cooler temperatures
and signs that summer
is fast fading.

A visitor from
California once
remarked that he had
never seen so many
different colors as in
Nebraska's countryside.

Baby pigs are some
of the cutest farm
animals. Nebraska is
seventh nationally in
the number of hogs and
pigs on farms.

Many Lincoln elementary school classes correspond with farm families through the "Ag in the Classroom" program and students sometimes visit nearby farms.

Three of every four Nebraska farms have livestock or poultry operations. Lancaster County has close to 40,000 hogs.

The whole family usually gets involved on that special night when spooks and goblins take to the streets.

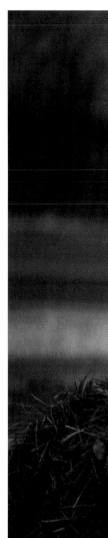

The setting for fall fun— campfires, s'mores, and ghost stories.

Wonder why retailers welcome Halloween? It's a good time of year to be in the candy business, too.

Every youngster has visions of someday playing like his favorite sports hero.

Fall means football. And in Lincoln that means

the Cornhuskers. And that means the heart beats faster

and the excitement reaches fever pitch.

Based on a photo of the 1995 Nebraska-Kansas State game, "Husker Legacy" was created by Lincoln artist Fred J. Hoppe and dedicated in September, 1997. The statue greets fans at the east entrance to Memorial Stadium.

The "Big Red Experience" is uniquely Nebraskan and something completely mysterious to most "outsiders."

Memorial Stadium is
not only a great place to
watch the Cornhuskers.
It's a great place to watch
the Cornhusker fans!

Introduced to Nebraska about 1915, the ring-necked pheasant is now established throughout the state. Nebraska hunters harvest nearly one-half million of the wary birds each year.

Nebraska Game and Park's Conservation Reserve Program—Management Access Program makes area farm fields available to hunters. With their purchases of hunting licenses, habitat stamps, firearms, and ammunition, hunters contribute over $13 million annually toward Game and Parks activities.

Fall is definitely an exhilarating time, both for hunters and their canine companions.

While Lincoln's skyline has changed some, it still retains the look of the "Prairie Capital."

Many historic homes dot Lincoln, including William Jennings Bryan's Fairview and the Thomas P. Kennard House, built in 1869 and home of Nebraska's first secretary of state.

Many areas within the city blend the look of old and new in a kind of eclectic neighborhood design.

Along with the Germans, Czechs, and Swedes of the 19th and 20th century immigrant waves, Nebraska and especially Lincoln have welcomed more recent refugees from places like Bosnia and the Ukraine.

Lincoln today still provides that "warm welcome" feeling to visitors and newcomers.

Many Lincoln citizens retain their family heritage, passed along from rural and small—town backgrounds.

Lincolnites are more casual nowadays, but they can be "formal" when the occasion requires. Casual or formal, Lincoln is made up of friendly folks.

chapter four

WINTER

L ast winter was unusual. No, it really was more a normal
winter. The winter before was unusual. But the winter
before that was more like the old winters. And so the discussion
goes on and on. The second greatest sport in Lincoln is trying
to guess what the forthcoming winter will be like!

No two winters are alike, especially in Nebraska. The past few
winters have been somewhat more moderate, but who knows
what the next one will bring? Lincoln's average snowfall is just
over 27 inches a year. But, it snowed 24 inches in 24 hours once
in 1965 and a total of 65 inches in 1948. In January, 1975, a
blizzard hit the capital city with 60 mph winds and wind chills
of 40 degrees below zero. Businesses closed at noon so workers
could get home before city busses stopped running. The storm
lasted just 24 hours but it brought the city to a standstill. Road
crews had trouble clearing highways because of stalled trucks
and cars, especially between Lincoln and Omaha.

Winter temperatures can be just about as variable. Average
high in January is 30.4 degrees. The average low is 8.9 degrees.
During the 1983 winter, the temperature stayed below zero for
188 hours (13 days). The city's coldest night was January 12,
1974, when the thermometer registered 33 degrees below zero.

Despite the uncertainty, winter doesn't really slow us down
much. In fact, Lincoln kicks off winter with a parade! The Star
City Holiday Parade gets the season rolling in early December.
And, when the snows and blows do kick in, kids and big kids
take out their ice skates and head to one of the local lakes or
ponds, or to the big ice skating rink at Mahoney State Park,
just a few miles up the road.

When the snows come, you'll find a lot of us out in it, some
cross-country skiing through Wilderness Park, others sledding
down Holmes Lake Dam or at Pioneers Park. Hardier souls will
take to the ice for ice fishing at one of the Salt Valley Lakes or
even at Holmes Lake after the trout are stocked.

Those that don't care to be out have plenty of activities
indoors. There are excellent programs at the Lied Center,
Community Playhouse, Kimball Hall, and the Star City Dinner
Theater. Both music and drama fans can find programs at other
venues around the city.

Winter can be variable. But Lincoln citizens take advantage
of whatever Mother Nature offers and make the best of it! ◼

With numerous acreages and "farmettes" around the city, Lancaster County actually has more farms (1,500) than any other county in the state.

Despite Lincoln's growing status as a cosmopolitan center, signs of the city's agricultural roots are never far away.

Lancaster County farmers generate more than $82 million in market value of farm products sold each year.

One of the great features
of Lincoln living is
the nearness of rural
surroundings. One can
get into the countryside
in a matter of minutes.

The city has many
faces—government,
university, financial
institutions—but the
nearby countryside is a
reminder that one of
every four Nebraskans
depends on agriculture
for employment.

Growth is making changes in the city's demographics,

but Lincoln is still a family town.

Lincoln has been a major railroad center since the city's early days, although many former railroad track beds are now part of Lincoln's trail system. Whether your passion is running, biking, rollerblading, or a leisurely walk, you can get around most of the city on Lincoln's extensive trails system. From south to north, several trails wind through neighborhoods and along city streets. For example, the MoPac trail leads from near City Campus east 20 miles through Walton to Elmwood, and eventually will hook up with the Platte River Connection near South Bend. Naturalist trails in Wilderness Park and the Pioneers Park Nature Center are popular with folks that enjoy viewing wildlife. Details? Check the Great Plains Trails Network Web site: www.gptn.org/trailinfo.htm.

Visitors are welcome at the Governor's Mansion and each year many area schoolchildren meet the governor and first lady in person.

Lincoln's skyline is sometimes said to "mirror" the natural pinnacles of the Panhandle, such as Chimney Rock.

Religion has always played a prominent role in Lincoln life. Many Lincoln churches are among the most historic buildings in the city.

*Now being restored,
the nine-and-a-half-ton
Sower was originally
hauled to the Capitol
Building by rail car on
specially built track to
the site. Carrying "the
seeds of life to be cast to
the winds," the Sower
represents agriculture,
Nebraska's main
industry, along with
acting as a lightning rod
for the Capitol. The
statue is nineteen feet
tall, made of half-inch
thick bronze, and has
graced the top of the
Capitol—400 feet
above the ground—
since 1930.*

The Capitol Rotunda is dedicated to human virtue. Eight angels holding hands in the ceiling—112 feet above the floor—represent the virtues of wisdom, justice, temperance, courage, faith, hope, charity, and magnanimity. The marble floor mosaic in the center is "Earth as the life-giver" and surrounding her are symbols of water, fire, air, and soil. The border surrounding the elements illustrates Nebraska's prehistoric life.

Builders saved the state money by building the new Nebraska Capitol around the old capitol building so state employees could continue working while the new structure was completed. The present structure is actually the third capitol building on the site, and was constructed over a ten-year period, from 1922-1932. The artistic plan for the Capitol was written by Hartley Burr Alexander in 1923.

Early Lincoln churches mostly represented the mainline denominations, but diversity in the city's culture and population has led to the establishment of more worship groups in recent years. At last count, Lincoln had at least 165 churches and two synagogues.

*Following the
1923 merger of two
congregations, First
Plymouth Congregational
Church was completed
and dedicated on
Easter Sunday,
April 5th, 1931.*

*Religious worship in Lincoln
ranges from casual to more formal,
but inspiring music, lessons, and
ritual are designed to appeal to
all ages and beliefs.*

Winter on the plains can be harsh at times, but nature's beauty shines through even when the thermometer dips.

*Many Lincolnites retain
their rural backgrounds
and welcome the chance
to experience the out-
doors, no matter what
the weather does.*

*Wildlife has learned
to adapt to populated
areas, sometimes moving
into the confines of the
city itself.*

part

TWO

CHAPTER FIVE

Transportation, Communications & Energy

Lincoln Electric System, 88-89 • Lincoln Airport, 90-91

One of the nation's leading utilities is located in Nebraska's capital city. The customer-owned Lincoln Electric System (LES) is nationally recognized for low costs, financial stability, innovation, and reliable, superior service.

In fact, as the new, competitive environment of deregulation began to develop in the industry, Wall Street analysts identified LES as one of 10 utilities best positioned to successfully compete in a restructured industry.

Low Energy Costs

An important factor in Lincoln's desirability as a business site is its low electric energy costs. Annual surveys by KPMG LLP have consistently found LES rates to be among the lowest 10 percent of average rates charged in the United States. This has prompted major businesses and manufacturers to choose Lincoln as a site to conduct business and manufacture products.

Fortune 500 and Global 500 organizations with Lincoln operations include State Farm Insurance Company, Pfizer Animal Health, Archer-Daniels-Midland Company, Goodyear Tire and Rubber Company, the Burlington Northern & Santa Fe Railway, and Kawasaki Motors Manufacturing Corp.

Financial Stability

Imagine living and working in a city where the price of electricity is as low today as it was 15 years ago. This is the reality enjoyed by more than 113,000 customers served by LES. Today, electric rates remain lower than in the mid-1980s.

Rates are kept low by controlling costs, particularly those for providing electric service to customers, which comprise 70 percent of total LES expenses. LES invests in some of the nation's most efficient and economical power plants, including Laramie River Station and Gerald Gentleman Station, two of the lowest-cost producers of steam-electric energy in the United States. Additionally, LES maintains strategic alliances with regional utilities to buy, sell, and transmit power when it is economically advantageous.

To ensure the future stability of energy costs, LES established a multi-million dollar Rate Stabilization Fund to cover unanticipated expenditures that could adversely affect customer electric rates. Management practices like these have earned Wall Street's respect. *Standard & Poors*, for example, cites LES' stable finances, strong business profile, competitive electric rates, and diverse, low-cost power resources as reasons for assigning its AA rating to the utility's revenue bonds.

LES invested $52 million in capital projects during 2000 to ensure that its power delivery system will reliably support loads and growth.

LES set the pace for Nebraska's energy innovation. It partnered with customers to fund, construct, and maintain two wind turbines under a program to promote the use of renewable resources.

Helping customers reduce their energy use and costs is a priority for the nonprofit LES. It provides many no-fee services to help customers make informed energy choices, including energy audits and evaluation of heating and cooling system needs.

Superior Service and Reliability

Changes in the structure of the electric utility industry have resulted in tight energy supplies and exorbitant energy costs for many utilities during the past few years. LES has avoided these adverse impacts by anticipating and planning for consequences of the industry's new, competitive environment, including innovative programs such as paying large customers to voluntarily reduce energy use during times of high customer demand.

Plans are in place to deal with the potential impacts of future industry deregulation as well. Chief among them is the acceleration of schedules to build more power generating facilities in the Lincoln area. These facilities will add about 247 megawatts of electricity to LES' power supplies. This additional capacity will help accommodate projected peak demand growth of 2.6 percent annually during the next decade.

The company invests millions of dollars in capital projects annually, including installation and upgrading or replacement of power lines and substations.

These high standards provide customers with exceptional reliability of electric service. In 2000, LES customers averaged only 10.8 minutes without electricity, a reliability level that exceeds 99.99 percent.

Known for Innovation

LES has been recognized nationally and internationally for its innovation. For example:

• LES partnered with the University of Nebraska-Lincoln to build a solar-assisted heat pump demonstration home in 1975, resulting in development of a patented technology for monitoring solar performance.

• In 1980, LES became the first utility in the nation to offer home energy audits under the National Energy Conservation Policy Act.

• LES has received the American Public Power Association's Energy Innovator Award twice. First in 1983 for developing comprehensive energy management strategies that benefited customers, and again in 1991

for conceiving a first-of-its-kind technology that increases the summer generating capacity of combustion turbines. These achievements have brought LES international acclaim.

LES continues to set the pace for energy innovation, especially in Nebraska. In 1998, it established a program to partner with customers to provide a portion of the energy used in its service area from renewable energy resources. By the end of 1999, two 660-kilowatt wind turbines were built and put into commercial operation. These wind turbines, combined with 30 percent ownership of two others built under the Nebraska Distributed Wind Energy Project, make LES the largest producer of wind energy in the state.

Striving for Excellence in the New Millennium

Achievements like these help LES fulfill its mission to provide energy and services of superior value to its customers and to enhance the growth and development of the greater Lincoln area. Be assured that LES will forge ahead to fulfill this mission in new and better ways in the years to come. ∎

LES customers do not face blackouts and high energy prices. They can rest assured that when they flip a switch, the energy they need will be there. One reason is LES' balanced mix of power resources. A local power peaking unit, Rokeby Unit No. 3 recently came online and provides 94 megawatts of generating capacity.

Thousands of Nebraskans are familiar with the Lincoln Airport, having flown into or out of it themselves, or their friends or family members have. Four major airlines presently serve Lincoln with 20 departing flights daily, including direct access to major hubs in Chicago, Denver, St. Louis, Minneapolis, and Kansas City.

Commercial aviation, however, is only a part of the Lincoln Airport story. Operated by the Lincoln Airport Authority, the airport hosts several general aviation operations, including air charter

LINCOLN AIRPORT

region. "There are businesses in Lincoln today because of our Air Park West facility," Wood says. "It is one of the most successful airport industrial parks in the nation."

In fact, Lincoln Airport has an economic impact on the community of nearly 3/4 billion dollars! Direct airport operations account for more than 2,700 jobs with an annual payroll of over $100 million. When indirect benefits and "multiplier" effects are added, the airport generates more like 7,100 jobs in the region and an annual payroll of $217 million. For comparison, a single employer of the same size would be one of the five largest employers in Lincoln.

Lincoln Airport is one of only two airports in Nebraska that receive no tax funding. Operating income from commercial airlines, charges and fees for facility use, and rental income from industrial park tenants fund all airport operations and maintenance of the facilities.

Aviation has played a part in Lincoln's development since the early 1900s. Charles Lindbergh took his first flying lessons here. The Goodyear plant in north Lincoln was once a manufacturing operation for the Arrow Sport Plane, an aerobatic biplane that once rolled off the Lincoln plant assembly line at the rate of five per day. An example of this sporty aircraft hangs in the airport terminal building.

Lincoln Airport had its beginnings in the early days of World War II. It was constructed in 1942 as Lincoln Air Base. Fighter pilots, bomber crews, and aviation mechanics were trained here throughout the war. Upwards of 65,000 personnel were processed through Lincoln Air Base for overseas duty. Hundreds more, both military and civilian, were employed at the base during the war years.

United, TWA, Northwest, and U.S. Airways Express serve Lincoln with over 20 flights per day. Photo by John F. Sanders

services and one of the country's largest corporate aircraft maintenance and modification facilities. Lincoln Airport also is home to two major military aircraft organizations, the Nebraska Air National Guard with its squadron of KC-135 tanker aircraft and an Army National Guard air ambulance helicopter unit. The airport's three runways (one of which is 2 1/2 miles long) also offer frequent support for U.S. Air Force flight training operations from Offutt Air Base near Omaha.

While the flight operations in and out of Lincoln Airport are more visible, many people aren't aware that Air Park West, located on the west side of the airport, is one of the largest airport industrial parks in the country. Also managed by the Lincoln Airport Authority, Air Park West covers some 1,280 acres and hosts more than 50 tenants. Tenants range from small start-up companies to branch and support facilities for major international firms.

"There are really two faces to the Lincoln Airport—the airport itself and the industrial park," says John Wood, Executive Director of the Lincoln Airport Authority. Both contribute greatly to the economic vitality of this

United Airlines' passengers checking in for a flight. Photo by John F. Sanders

The base was deactivated at the end of the war. The facilities were adapted for commercial use and for the Air Guard. However, a defense build-up during the Cold War led to reactivation of the base in 1954, under the Strategic Air Command. Two wings of B-47 bombers and their support crews were stationed at the base. Later, the base became the headquarters for Atlas and Nike missile installations in the area. The base was again deactivated in 1966 and transferred to the city, under the Lincoln Airport Authority.

The airport still serves a valuable military function, as home base for the Nebraska Air Guard and Army Guard aviation units, and frequent support for U.S. Air Force training and as a standby facility.

Lincoln Airport's terminal complex was completed in 1975 and expanded in 1988. The terminal complex was designed with a weathered steel, glass, and brick exterior to provide a dramatic architectural addition to the airport proper. The terminal is a modern combination of sound functional planning and centrally located public services, all with a bright, warm decor. The unique design gives passengers the shortest possible distance from auto to airplane, in contrast to many airports around the country.

Covering 5,500 acres of rolling Nebraska prairie, Lincoln Airport has become a tremendous asset to the Lincoln area and indeed much of Southeast Nebraska. Both commercial and general aviation operations continue to expand as Lincoln grows. And, Lincoln Air Park West continues to grow as more and more companies find the old air base an ideal location for their operations.

The purpose of the Lincoln Airport Authority is to ensure that the entire airport keeps pace with the increasing demands of the local community, both for air transportation and for business expansion.

According to Executive Director John Wood, Lincoln Airport will continue to meet its objectives as a major transportation center and "job generator" for Lincoln, and a vital contributor to the overall economy of the area. ■

Duncan Aviation is one of the top corporate aircraft maintenance and modification centers in the world and employs some 1,500 people at its Lincoln operation. Photo by John F. Sanders

The Lincoln Airport Terminal, constructed in 1975, is a very open functional design which allows for easy passenger access to aircraft loading areas. Photo by John F. Sanders

CHAPTER SIX

Manufacturing & Distribution

The largest manufacturing site for Pfizer animal health products is right here in Lincoln, Nebraska. Pfizer Inc is a global, research-based pharmaceutical company known the world over for such advanced medicines as Lipitor®, Celebrex®, Viagra®, Zoloft®, Aricept®, Zyrtec®, Zithromax®, Norvasc®, and others. Most consumers are familiar with Pfizer's consumer brands—Benadryl®, Listerine®, Neosporin®, Visine®, BenGay®, Schick®, and many more. Veterinarians, livestock producers and pet owners are probably more familiar with Pfizer's biological and pharmaceutical products for cattle, swine, horses, dogs, and cats.

When veterinarian Carl Norden founded the operations in Lincoln in 1919, he could not have anticipated its growth to such worldwide prominence. Carl Norden was born in Sweden, and came to the United States with his parents in the early 1900s. After his graduation from Kansas City Veterinary College in 1911, Dr. Norden worked in a private veterinary practice in Nebraska City. He served as a lieutenant in the U.S. Army's Veterinary Corps during World War I, after which he returned to Nebraska and became Assistant State Veterinarian. It was this exposure to the need for better veterinary service for livestock producers that led Norden to start his own business which, for the next 70 years, would be known as Norden Laboratories.

Growth of the business was steady for the next several decades. By 1927, Dr. Norden was beginning to develop his own line of biological products. Norden Laboratories acquired Platte Valley Serum Company in 1934 and the expanded company soon became known as the premier supplier of hog cholera serum. By 1959, 40 years after its start, the company's product line included some 280 biological and pharmaceutical products, being marketed throughout the country and in 24 other countries.

Norden Laboratories became a subsidiary of Smith Kline & French Laboratories in 1959, which later became SmithKline Beckman. A new facility was opened in 1967 on a 145-acre site in northwest Lincoln. Several expansions since then have added more than 700,000 square feet to the operation, including a state-of-the-art bulk biologicals plant in 1994. The 1970s and 1980s were banner years for the company. The business enjoyed steady growth as many highly successful products were introduced and more sophisticated manufacturing methods and equipment were implemented.

In the virus production laboratory at Pfizer, a technician harvests virus fluid from a container in which the virus has been grown. The fluid is one of the components for some of the many vaccines Pfizer produces to aid in the prevention of disease. Photo by John F. Sanders

Pfizer's Lincoln Operation produces more than 550 million viral and bacterin vaccine doses every year. Biological products include *RespiSure®* for preventing respiratory disease in swine, *Bovi-Shield®* for prevention of respiratory and reproductive disease in cattle, and the *Vanguard®* line of products for prevention of canine enteric disease. Biological products produced in Lincoln are exported to more than 65 countries.

Pfizer pharmaceutical products for the animal health industry produced in Lincoln include *Rimadyl®* for treating osteoarthritis in dogs, *Anipryl®* for treatment of Cushing's disease and Cognitive Dysfunction Syndrome in dogs, *Pet-Tabs®* vitamins for cats and dogs, and *Anthelcide®* EQ for treating parasites in horses. Annual production volume is: More than 500,000 liters of liquid, over 1.5 million kilograms of solids, and more than 600 million tablets.

Pfizer operations in Lincoln today occupy nearly 900,000 square feet of laboratory, office, and manufacturing space. Pfizer is one of Lincoln's top industrial employers, with more than 800 employees.

In Pfizer's pharmaceutical production area, a packaging operator monitors the paste packaging line. Photo by John F. Sanders

Two name changes for the operation took place in the late 1900s. In 1989, the site became known as SmithKline Beecham Animal Health with the merger of SmithKline Beckman and Beecham Laboratories. In 1995, the site became part of Pfizer Inc when Pfizer purchased the SmithKline Beecham Animal Health business.

Pfizer's Lincoln Operations remains focused on manufacturing technology, combining scientific expertise with dedication to continuous improvement. It is poised for the promise and challenge of the future. Pfizer is a world leader in research and development dedicated to animal health. The number of product candidates in the pipeline has increased significantly in recent years, and Pfizer Lincoln is expected to become the manufacturing site for some of these new products.

As a major Lincoln employer, Pfizer contributes greatly to the economic vitality of the community. The company also is a major contributor to Lincoln's many community service activities, especially in health care, education, community, and cultural affairs. Pfizer Lincoln employees have repeatedly been among the largest contributors to the Lincoln/Lancaster County United Way/CHAD campaign. Pfizer employees also contribute their time to a wide range of community betterment activities, such as the local Paint-A-Thon and Junior Achievement.

Pfizer is a strong supporter of math and science education in local schools through the Pfizer Education Initiative, which includes an annual Pfizer/LPS Science

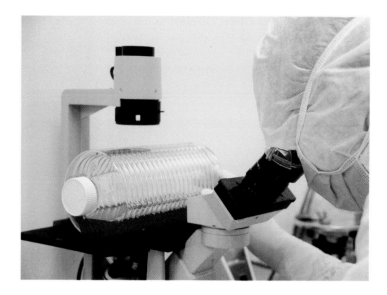

Fair and Ventures in Partnership support for West Lincoln Elementary School. In 1999, Pfizer Lincoln dedicated a restored 25-acre saline wetland on its property that is open for public use. The wetland's interpretive walking trail includes educational exhibits and information.

Pfizer Lincoln proudly accepted the Mayor's first annual Community Conscience Award in 2000 for its outstanding record as a corporate citizen. The award recognized Pfizer's role in supporting nonprofit organizations and the company's participation in building a healthy Lincoln community. ■

A virus production laboratory technician examines cultured cells via a microscope during the virus production process. Photo by John F. Sanders

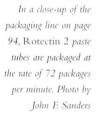

In a close-up of the packaging line on page 94, Rotectin 2 *paste tubes are packaged at the rate of 72 packages per minute. Photo by John F. Sanders*

The Goodyear Tire & Rubber Company is a long-running contributor to the vitality of the Lincoln area and the state of Nebraska. With its Engineered Products manufacturing facility in Havelock and its Global Distribution Center at Lincoln Airpark West, Goodyear has contributed $120 million annually to the local area economy. Amazingly, nearly 13,000 people have worked for Goodyear-Lincoln over the years.

It all began in 1943 when Goodyear headquarters in Akron, Ohio leased a 100,000-square-foot building in Havelock to manufacture self-sealing fuel tanks for World War II aircraft. The tanks were designed to

absorb multiple bullet punctures without exploding. Appropriately enough, the building had previously been used by another early Lincoln firm, the Arrow Aircraft Company, to build small planes.

The plant was closed after the war ended, but Goodyear re-opened the plant in 1946 to produce V-belts. Shortly thereafter, Goodyear-Lincoln began manufacturing flat belts for the new Allis Chalmers Roto-Baler, one of the earliest concepts in making round hay bales. Eventually, the Goodyear product line included more heavy-duty V-belts, combine cylinder belts, and variable speed traction drive belts.

Over the years, Goodyear-Lincoln has supplied much of the country's agricultural industry. Tractors and combines that have employed Goodyear belts and hoses include John Deere, Case, International, Hesston, Massey Ferguson, and others. Most of today's farm machinery uses Goodyear products to transmit power or coolant for smoother operation. Other firms such as Cargill, ADM, Farmland Industries, and Pioneer are major users of Goodyear industrial power transmission products. More specialized Goodyear products are used on potato harvesters, fruit and vegetable sorting lines, mechanical sweet corn harvesters, and in cotton gins.

In 1950, Goodyear-Lincoln added curved radiator hose production for the auto industry and the plant was doubled in size to 200,000 square feet. Positive drive belts were added to the product mix in 1956 and poly V-belts (serpentine belts) went into production in 1961. After several more plant expansions in the 1960s and

Above: Goodyear's Global Distribution Center at Lincoln Airpark. Photo by John F. Sanders

Goodyear's Engineered Products Plant. Photo by John F. Sanders

1970s, the Goodyear facility covered more than 1,000,000 square feet—the largest Goodyear industrial products manufacturing facility in the world! Goodyear remains one of Lincoln's largest industrial employers.

Today, Goodyear-Lincoln includes the national marketing headquarters for Replacement Products, Hose, and Power Transmission Products. The worldwide computer information system for Engineered Products is housed here. And, the operation serves as Worldwide Power Transmission Products Technical Center for Goodyear, developing products, process, and production machinery used by other Goodyear plants around the world.

The company's Global Distribution Center (GDC) at Airpark incorporates products from the Lincoln facility as well as other operations at Norfolk, Nebraska, Mt. Pleasant, Iowa, and other plants. The GDC in turn supplies products to dealers across the country and distribution outlets around the world.

In 1981, Goodyear purchased the former Havelock School building and created the Goodyear Fitness Center, just six blocks away from the Goodyear-Lincoln plant. The fitness center is designed to enhance the health of Goodyear employees and their families, and is open on a limited basis to the general public. Although most of the fitness center users are Goodyear families, nearly 25 percent of the regular customers are not associated with the company.

The Goodyear Daycare Center was opened next door to the fitness center in 1986. The day care center, now

Display of Patent Awards to Goodyear Associates. Photo by John F. Sanders

called the Goodyear Early Learning Center, provides employees and other fitness center members with convenient, professional care for their children from 8 weeks to 11 years old during weekday working hours.

During its more than 55 years in Lincoln, Goodyear has been a major supporter of local community activities and charitable organizations. In fact, it was a former Goodyear-Lincoln plant manager, Dan Remigio, who got the local Junior Achievement program going in 1971. Since then, thousands of area young people have been exposed to the basics of business and marketing. And Goodyear-Lincoln still donates use of one of its buildings for Junior Achievement activities.

Goodyear staff and employees are active in numerous community youth programs, such as Big Brothers-Big Sisters, 4-H, Little League, Boy Scouts, Girl Scouts, and others. Each year, Goodyear volunteers help with the Lincoln Public Schools "Ventures in Partnership" program and work with human service organizations like the March of Dimes, Juvenile Diabetes Foundation, and the Lincoln Action Program.

Goodyear-Lincoln associates in 2000 pledged over one-quarter million dollars to the local United Way/ CHAD. Since 1990, Goodyear associates have donated enough food to the Lincoln Food Pantry to feed the entire population of Beatrice. Just in the past two years, Goodyear's on-site blood drive has collected enough blood to save 2,000 lives!

Today's Goodyear-Lincoln operation remains the flagship of the Goodyear Engineered Products Division. The plant has received numerous top-quality awards from customers like GM, Chrysler, Toyota, Navistar, Toro, Saturn, and others. The employee/associates of Goodyear-Lincoln continually exhibit a "can-do" spirit and attitude in both their work responsibilities and their community activities.

It all adds up to making Goodyear-Lincoln an outstanding corporate citizen. ■

Goodyear Fitness Center. Photo by John F. Sanders

When Dorsey Laboratories moved into its new facility on Highway 6, east of Lincoln, the building occupied 166,000 square feet and was cited as one of the "Top 10 New Plants" by Factory Magazine. That was 1963.

Today, the pharmaceutical manufacturing facility covers more than 400,000 square feet and an associated Midwest Distribution Center occupies another 108,000 square feet.

The Lincoln operation began in 1908, when three pharmaceutical salesmen formed the Smith-Dorsey Company. They began operations in a rented office in a three-story building at 113 South 10th Street. (The

Terminal Building at the corner of 10th and O eventually replaced this building.) A year later, the firm moved to larger spaces at 210 South 12th Street. The company now occupied an area 25 feet wide by 75 feet long, with an office at the front, stock room in the center, and a shipping room at the back.

By 1916, company sales were $33,000 and all the original owners had left the company. The new owners retained the Smith Dorsey name. During the early 1920s, a young University of Nebraska student worked at Smith-Dorsey part time to help pay her education costs. Later, she wrote a novel in which one of the characters worked for a wholesale drug firm in Lincoln. The author: Mari Sandoz.

The Wander Company acquired the Smith-Dorsey Company in the early 1950s. The merger provided additional operating funds for scientific research and helped lead to the development of Triaminic® tablets in 1956. With some changes, that original formula has been manufactured by a number of affiliated companies around the globe.

The company name was changed to Dorsey Laboratories in 1960. A few years later, after the move to the new building on Highway 6, the Wander Company was merged with Sandoz Ltd. When Sandoz and Ciba-Geigy merged to form Novartis AG in 1997, the Lincoln operation became a part of Novartis Consumer Health, Inc.

Above: Novartis Consumer Health, Inc. Photo courtesy of Novartis Consumer Health

Analysts in the Quality Services laboratory perform numerous checks on both raw materials and finished products to ensure the quality of Novartis products. Photo by John F. Sanders

Today, Novartis' Lincoln operation includes two manufacturing areas, one focused on liquids/semi-solids and the other on making solids. The operation also includes a nationwide distribution center for Novartis Consumer Health.

Products made in Lincoln include syrups, suspensions, creams, softgel capsules, tablets, and granules. Such well-known products as Triaminic®, TheraFlu®, Tavist®, Maalox®, and Lamisil^AT™ Cream are made and packaged here. Some prescription pharmaceuticals and animal health products for the U.S. are also manufactured at Lincoln. More than 70 million units are packaged every year.

Recent new products include Triaminic® Softchews™ tablets, launched nationwide in 1999, and Maalox® Quick Dissolve tablets, introduced in 1999 in recognition of the 50th birthday of the Maalox® brand. Lamisil^AT™ Cream was switched from prescription to over-the-counter status and contains the only OTC ingredient that cures athlete's foot with just one week of treatment.

The Lincoln operation employs approximately 500 full-time workers, as well as a seasonal workforce. The plant operates in a team-based environment with three shifts, five days a week.

Novartis provides excellent company benefits for its associates, including medical, dental, life, vision and legal insurance, child care and elder care assistance, 401(K), pension plan, and educational assistance. The Lincoln plant includes a company-subsidized cafeteria,

Triaminic® line of products. Photo by John F. Sanders

fitness center, and tennis courts, and sponsors a wide range of recreational opportunities and intramural sports teams for associates.

On a corporate level and individually, Novartis and its associates actively support the Lincoln community, contributing time and money to nearly 60 charitable organizations, including refurbishing of the Zooville Square at Folsom Children's Zoo, and participating in Lincoln Public Schools "Ventures in Partnership" program. The company also joins with the Lincoln Track Club each spring to sponsor the Novartis Run.

The Novartis Foundation has made major contributions to the Teammates Mentoring Program in Lincoln and the YMCA Building Fund.

Lincoln's Novartis Consumer Health is part of a world-leading healthcare company with core businesses in pharmaceuticals, consumer health, generics, eye care, and animal health. Almost 68,000 workers around the globe manufacture and market the many products that bear the Novartis name. The company's well-known and trusted brands include Gerber®, Maalox®, Triaminic®, and Ex-Lax®.

Novartis shares began trading on the New York Stock Exchange in May 2000, as American Depository Shares. Trades are listed under the symbol "NVS." ■

Tavist® line of products. Photo by John F. Sanders

Many of Lincoln's citizens aren't aware of it, but a local manufacturing operation is a key player in the global high-tech industry. Molex, with three Lincoln locations and a workforce of more than 700 skilled workers, supplies critical components to industries worldwide.

Lincoln's Molex facilities are part of a global network of 50 manufacturing operations in 21 countries. Worldwide headquarters are located in Lisle, Illinois. Molex produces electrical, electronic, and fiber optic connectors for the telephone, cellular phone, electric power, and computer industries. Connector products and systems, switches, and assemblies are manufactured for the automotive and appliance industries. The company provides products and components to such multinational firms as IBM, Intel, Chrysler, Compaq, Motorola, Hewlett Packard, AT&T, and Whirlpool.

Lincoln's "Upland" facility on Kingbird Road has the distinction of being one of the largest Molex manufacturing facilities, as well as one of the most technologically advanced. The company operates with a "Total Quality Management" philosophy, including input from employee teams. In fact, employee ideas were included when the new Upland plant was built in 1994, and when new additions were added in 1996 and 2000. The plant has a unique layout, which facilitates efficient manufacturing processes and a clean, modern work environment.

The Upland plant also was one of five U.S. manufacturing facilities selected for an Environmental Protection Agency waste-handling project in 1998. As a result of

that project, Molex waste products from manufacturing processes are segregated into specific elements (nickel, copper, tin/lead), substantially reducing the amount of heavy metals going into waste treatment facilities and increasing the amount of materials that are recycled.

Another example of the high-tech aspect of Molex manufacturing facilities in Lincoln is the company's recent implementation of "Fast Component Manufacturing" (FCM). Capacitors used in automotive connectors are assembled on a flat-flex coil, using the

"fastest pick-and-place operation in the world." The unique process was developed as a joint venture between Molex and other multinational companies, Philips and Sheldahl.

Molex first came to Lincoln in 1977 with its plant on West Bond, where automotive products are assembled. New automobiles today contain numerous Molex connectors for such sophisticated instrumentation as global navigation systems, ABS brakes, and airbags, as well as specialized connectors for power trains, comfort controls, and entertainment systems. Molex also is the leading connector supplier to the major appliance manufacturers.

Worldwide, Molex reached the $2 billion mark in sales in 2000. With more than 500,000 square feet of manufacturing space and its highly skilled workforce, Lincoln's Molex facilities will continue to be an important part of the company's future growth. Molex will continue to be a key element in Lincoln's economic growth as well. ■

Molex stamping department. Photo by John F. Sanders

Molex-Lincoln component plant at 700 Kingbird Road. Photo by John F. Sanders

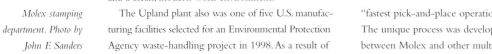

When Kawasaki established its Lincoln plant in 1974, many Kawasaki products that have become so popular today were still on the drawing boards. Other products were yet to be designed.

The initial Lincoln facility was designed for the assembly of Kawasaki motorcycles, and the first one came off the assembly line in January, 1975. By mid-1975, production of the Jet Ski®, a personal watercraft that has captured the attention of fun lovers the world over, was underway at Lincoln.

KAWASAKI MOTORS MANUFACTURING CORP., U.S.A.

ATV engines for Kawasaki units and Deere lawnmowers. ATV wheel rims are produced in Lincoln, for Kawasaki ATVs and several other manufacturers.

State-of-the-art industrial robots also are built in Lincoln and marketed throughout the world to companies like Ford Motor Company, as well as being used in other Kawasaki plants. The robots are used for a variety of jobs such as handling molten aluminum for making die-cast crankcases.

The Lincoln plant achieved ISO 9002 certification for manufacturing industrial robots in 1995. The Maryville operation achieved ISO 9002 status in 1999, for its production of small engines.

Kawasaki Motors Manufacturing Corp., U.S.A. is strongly employee oriented. A flexible workflow technique and worker input have led to an innovative manufacturing process called the Kawasaki Production System (KPS). KPS has been so successful that many other manufacturers visit Lincoln to learn about the system.

"Club K," an in-plant fitness center, is available to all Lincoln employees and their spouses. The center is designed to promote wellness and physical fitness through personalized workout programs. ■

Mixed model assembly lowers inventory requirements and allows Kawasaki to meet customer demand.

Kawasaki 2001 VN800/Vulcan Classic Motorcycle.

Other products followed: ATV production in 1980, manufacture of ATV wheels in 1986, production of utility vehicles (the "Mule") in 1987, building small industrial engines in 1989 (Maryville plant), assembly of ATV engines in 1991, machining and assembly of robotic arms in 1994, and now, starting in 2002, manufacture of light rail cars for mass transit systems in cities around the country.

Kawasaki Motors Manufacturing Corp., U.S.A. now operates a modern Lincoln facility that covers more than 1 1/4 million square feet and employs approximately 1,000 workers. An associated facility in Maryville, Missouri, covers almost 3/4 million square feet and has over 400 workers. When the new rail car facility is completed, just south of the main plant on Northwest 27th Street, it will add another 430,000 square feet of space and an estimated 300 more employees.

Lincoln's Kawasaki plant still produces motorcycles— and, with the Maryville facility—produces all-terrain vehicles, Jet Ski® watercraft, and utility vehicles for 1,200 independent dealerships nationwide. The Maryville plant also builds small engines for lawn, garden, turf, and commercial applications, including

In 1885, brothers Frank and George Steiner, just nine and 12 years old, delivered clean towels to taverns and eating establishments along O Street in downtown Lincoln. The brothers used the back room of their Uncle Charles Rohman's delicatessen to store their towel and apron supplies.

Charles' son, Carl P. Rohman, started a linen supply business in Colorado Springs a few years later. Charles' other son, George W. Rohman, bought Root Towel in Lincoln

1967. The company moved to its new facility on North 41st Street in 1968, where it headquarters today, and the company name was changed to Uniservice, reflecting the addition of the Hastings and Omaha facilities.

Uniservice has won industry awards for its building layout and workspace design, which introduced ergonomics before the term was even well recognized. The company was one of the first to employ computers in the linen supply industry, and established a separate computer service (Unisystems) in the late 1960s to provide computer services to companies throughout the industry. Although the computer business was sold in 1983, the company still uses a sophisticated computer and bar code system to track and sort garments.

Uniservice today serves over 3,500 customers throughout Nebraska, from Lincoln and from the branch offices in Omaha and Hastings. The firm is a full service provider of industrial, health care and food preparation garments, table linens, floor mats, etc. Uniservice provides tablecloths and napkins for local restaurants, linens for local hotels and motels, and towels and uniforms for local health care, service firms, and industrial operations.

The company has continued to grow and now employs a workforce of 115 people, many of whom have been with Uniservice for 20 to 30 years. Average tenure is 11 years, according to General Manager Stephen Rohman. Stephen is the third generation of the family to manage the business. ∎

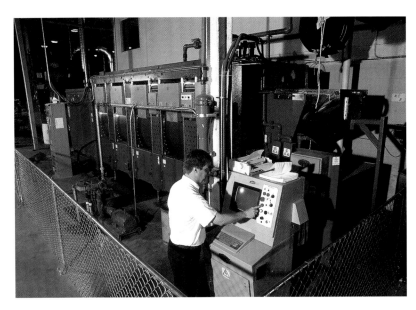

Uniservice uses state-of-the-art washing technology.

and combined it with two other firms to form Sanitary Towel & Laundry in 1912. They moved the new company into a building at 2019 N Street. The building is still there, with the faded "Sanitary Towel & Laundry" visible on the building facade. Carl P. sold his business in Colorado Springs in 1914 and returned to Lincoln to join the firm.

Carl H. Rohman, son of Carl P., worked for the company as a youngster and had just begun law school at UNL when World War II started. He ended up as an artillery forward observer and took part in the Battle of the Bulge. After the war, he returned to finish law school and eventually take over the company.

By the early 1960s, the business had expanded into five separate buildings near 19th and N Streets. A Hastings firm, Modern Linens, was acquired in 1965 and Frontier Linens in Omaha was acquired in

Uniservice's distinctive trucks are seen throughout the state.

CHAPTER SEVEN

Business, Finance & The Professions

While the Wells Fargo stage-coach logo is relatively new to Nebraska, the company behind it has a long history of service to the state. Henry Wells and William G. Fargo founded Wells, Fargo & Co. in 1852 to provide express and banking services to the Gold Rush West.

Although the early offices were in San Francisco and Sacramento, Wells Fargo soon established agencies and express routes across the Western plains and mountains. Wells Fargo opened its first express office in Nebraska in 1867.

The enclosed garden courtyard is used for a variety of community exhibits and displays. Photo by John F. Sanders

The company established direct "Ocean-to-Ocean" service in 1888, and by the early 20th century, Wells Fargo had more than 10,000 offices nationwide. It also set up large banking offices in New York and major cities of the West.

The Wells Fargo bank network today is one of the largest in the country, with banking operations in 23 states and nearly 6,000 bank and financial centers. Since its merger with Norwest and acquisition of First Commerce Bancshares (National Bank of Commerce in Lincoln and six Greater Nebraska banks), Wells Fargo is now Nebraska's second largest bank network, with 48 store locations and over 180 ATMs throughout the state.

While Wells Fargo is no longer in the express business, it is much more than just a bank. Today, Wells Fargo is a diversified financial services company that provides banking, insurance, investments, mortgage, and consumer finance services across North America and overseas. The company is rated number one in the industry in many areas, including small business lending, agricultural lending, commercial real estate lending, mortgage origination, and online financial services. Wells Fargo is the country's second largest SBA lender.

In its October, 2000 issue, Global Finance named Wells Fargo the "Best Bank" in the United States, based on performance over the past year and other subjective criteria such as reputation and management excellence. The magazine's editors made the selection after extensive consultation with bankers, analysts, and corporate financial executives throughout the world.

"This is a great honor for our company because we earned it in the midst of one of the most complex conversions in banking history," said Dick Kovacevich, Wells Fargo President and CEO. "It confirms that in the opinion of a select group of experts Wells Fargo is number one, second to none in satisfying our customers' financial needs and helping them succeed financially."

Lincoln's Wells Fargo stores are part of the USA's largest contiguous banking franchise, with nearly 3,000 community banking stores and over 24 million customer households throughout the western two-thirds of the country. Wells Fargo has 120,000 team members nationwide.

Wells Fargo banking operations in Lincoln have a rich history, as the National Bank of Commerce. The company was founded in 1902 and has always been located at the corner of 13th and O Streets, although not always on the same corner! The NBC Center (now Wells Fargo Center) on the northwest corner of 13th and O, was built in 1976.

The 12-story, block-long structure became an instant architectural landmark for Lincoln. Designed by noted New York architect I. M. Pei, the building was designed so that, viewed from the east side, the structure resembles the outline of the state of Nebraska.

The Wells Fargo Center, designed by noted architect I.M. Pei, resembles the outline of the state of Nebraska. Photo by John F. Sanders

Wells Fargo is a diversified financial services company that provides banking, insurance, investments, mortgages, and consumer finance services to its customers. Photo by John F. Sanders

Wells Fargo bank operations occupy about one-half of the building, including part of the concourse area and the first five floors. Various groups and organizations lease the other offices in the 300,000-square-foot building. Because of its architectural status, cosmetic changes to the building must be approved by Lincoln's Historic Preservation Commission.

The first-floor atrium level of the Wells Fargo Center was designed specifically for the convenience of customers and pedestrians. The lobby offers indoor passage from O Street to P Street, convenient when outdoor weather is uncomfortable.

The enclosed garden courtyard on the bank's main level was designed especially for community use. The courtyard is used for various art exhibits, quilt and sculpture displays, senior center craft exhibits, and other events. The adjacent outdoor plaza is also available for community use, hosting music groups and other special community activities from time to time. Centerpiece of the enclosed courtyard is the 20-foot-tall *ficus-nitida* tree, a member of the fig family. The tree, now over 45 years old, was incorporated into the original design of the building and the indoor courtyard.

Wells Fargo Bank has a strong commitment to the Lincoln community. For years, Wells Fargo has been a major contributor to numerous community activities and charitable organizations. Each year, Wells Fargo awards thousands of dollars to cultural venues and activities, educational institutions and groups, religious organizations, and human service activities.

Whether it is investing in a small business to create more jobs, helping economically disadvantaged families become more self-sufficient, or helping low-income families become home-owners, Wells Fargo seeks to serve. Likewise, Wells Fargo team members are active in volunteer organizations and activities that promote the betterment of the Lincoln community.

The Wells Fargo vision is to be the premier financial services company in Lincoln and throughout Nebraska, and to lead the way in corporate citizenship for making our community a better place to live—the same goals the original Wells Fargo Company had when it first came to Nebraska back in 1867. ■

Wells Fargo team members are active in volunteer organizations and activities that promote the betterment of the Lincoln community. Photo by John F. Sanders

From a company that began in 1938, offering burial insurance coverage for $1 per month, Lincoln Benefit Life has grown to become a major national force in the life insurance industry. The company provides protection, security, and service to individuals and sales producers across the U.S., in Puerto Rico, and in Guam.

Lincoln Benefit Life was acquired by Sears in 1981. Now as a member of Allstate Financial Group, Lincoln Benefit Life is backed by one of the industry's strongest financial and insurance companies, Allstate Life Insurance Company.

product line to meet the changing needs of its policyholders. In 1994, the company introduced variable universal life insurance and variable annuity products. A few short years after introduction, the variable life product line grew to rank 18th in the life insurance industry.

Entering the new century, Lincoln Benefit Life insures more than 770,000 policyholders with over $120 billion face-value in life insurance protection. It offers key products for both personal and business risk management and financial planning, including family protection, estate and retirement planning, and business continuity planning.

These competitively-priced life insurance and annuity products are available through a network of 105,000 independent insurance producers who are professionals in their own right. The products appeal to independent-minded individuals who prefer to make their own, informed choices.

Lincoln Benefit Life continues to grow and gain new business because of its four-fold promise to policy holders: value, service, strength, and innovation.

• Value includes those high-quality insurance solutions to personal and business needs that provide solid, affordable insurance for the policyholder's investment.

• Service is the company's commitment to give each policyholder clear, honest, personal dedication to meeting that person's needs as they change with time and growth.

• Strength is Lincoln Benefit Life's performance as an efficient, well-run company that is financially solid and highly rated within the insurance industry.

• Innovation entails all those unique insurance solutions and cutting-edge plans that are the on-going hallmark of Lincoln Benefit Life, and that enhance continued growth and success.

Lincoln Benefit Life's new facilities sport scenic views. Photo by John F. Sanders

Growth has always played a role in the company's history since its founding in a small Lincoln office. Within decades, it grew to become a well-respected community leader settled in its own 12-story office structure on the corner of 13th and O streets in downtown Lincoln. After it spread into five separate locations, in 1999 Lincoln Benefit Life moved its staff, that now numbers more than 700, to a 24-acre campus in southeast Lincoln.

Its two new three-story buildings with over 180,000 square feet include a 250-seat cafeteria and a 24-hour employee fitness center. Outdoors is a 5,000-square-foot patio. A walking-running track surrounds the campus, which has space set aside for construction of a proposed third office structure. The campus at 84th and Van Dorn is bordered on three sides by Firethorn Golf Club.

Lincoln Benefit Life's growth is measured by more than brick and mortar. Financially, the company has produced an enviable record. Its $63 million in assets in 1981 jumped to $5 billion by 1994. In 2000, company assets reached $9 billion. Fixed life insurance and annuities were its foundation products through the early years. Since then, Lincoln Benefit Life has successfully expanded its

Applications are scanned for electronic storage and a "paperless" workplace. Photo by John F. Sanders

Lincoln Benefit Life is a charter member of the Insurance Marketplace Standards Association (IMSA), a voluntary membership organization formed in 1998, and dedicated to maintain high ethical standards for advertising, sales, and service in the life insurance marketplace. As an IMSA member, Lincoln Benefit Life announces its commitment to honesty, fairness, and integrity in all contacts with policyholders involving sales and service of life insurance and annuity products.

Lincoln Benefit Life has been highly rated by the industry's independent analytical services. A.M. Best, Standard & Poor's, and Moody's, the acknowledged leaders for evaluating the financial condition and claims-paying ability of insurance companies, give Lincoln Benefit Life some of their highest ratings for financial stability and strength.

As one of Lincoln's top 10 employers, Lincoln Benefit Life maintains a strong commitment to the local community. The company's overall corporate philosophy includes "giving back" to Lincoln so that the community continues to thrive as a home for its employees. Along with its contributions to the arts and local programs like the Cornhusker State Games, the company is a major benefactor of the Lincoln Children's Museum.

The company strongly supports employee volunteerism, and nearly three-quarters of Lincoln Benefit Life staff members volunteer for some type of community activity. Always strong supporters of the company-sponsored charitable giving campaign, employee participation reached an outstanding 93 percent in 2000. Many employees serve on boards and committees of service programs throughout the local community.

The Lincoln Benefit Life staff approaches these responsibilities in much the same way they approach their everyday tasks as representatives of Lincoln Benefit Life. That's why, through the years, Lincoln Benefit Life has earned the reputation for exceptional personal service to its producers and its policyholders.

Just as it did in the past, the company has established very aggressive growth goals for the near future. As it continues to grow, Lincoln Benefit Life also keeps an important, customer-oriented goal in focus: Help our clients save for retirement, provide financial security for their loved ones, fund their children's education, and support new business ventures. ■

Employees enjoy a full service cafeteria and patio seating. Photo by John F. Sanders

A teamwork environment helps Lincoln Benefit Life achieve its business goals. Photo by John F. Sanders

Lincoln's Staybridge Suites offers the perfect extended stay accommodations for both business and leisure travelers. A new concept developed by Holiday Inn®, Staybridge Suites is the ultimate all-suite hotel, offering studio, one bedroom, and two bedroom/two bath floor plans. Each of its 109 suites includes a fully equipped kitchen, a work area, living room, and sleeping area. Also, every suite is furnished with the best in ergonomic and comfortable furniture, including an oversized desk.

Additionally, Staybridge Suites offers an around-the-clock convenience store with snacks, beverages, frozen foods, toiletries, and other essentials. There is a free self-service laundry room, fitness center, and an outside courtyard area with barbecue grills, pool, and spa. Lincoln's Staybridge Suites opened in October 1999 and has the distinction of being the first franchise in the world for this newest of traveler accommodation concepts. There are more than 35 new Staybridge Suites under construction and Holiday Inn expects to have at least 250 of the facilities open by 2005. The Lincoln operation provides year-round employment for 30 persons.

Staybridge Suites is located just south of I-80 on North 27th Street at Fletcher Avenue. The location provides convenient access to all parts of Lincoln, as well as timesaving access to the interstate for travelers headed east or west. Several restaurants and shopping areas also are nearby. The Lincoln operation is owned by a partnership of local investors. For information, visit www.sbs-lincoln.com. For locations of other Staybridge Suites, or to make reservations, check www.staybridge.com/lincoln1-80.

Staybridge Suites brings to Lincoln a luxurious setting for the visitor and business traveler, with unique amenities that enable guests to work in a productive environment and enjoy the comfort of pleasant surroundings as well. ■

Staybridge Suites, located at North 27th and Fletcher Avenue. Photo by John F. Sanders

Staybridge Suites offers unique amenities, as well, including two phone lines in each suite with customized voice mail, along with a separate dataport connection for high-speed Internet access. Guests can work online from the privacy of their own suite or visit the main floor Guest Library and use one of the hotel's workstations with high-speed Internet access. Staybridge's Business Center has a laser printer, available through each room's Internet connection, enabling guests to print out hard copies from their own suite. The Business Center fax machine and copier are available 24 hours a day for guest use.

Guests have a choice of a complimentary hot breakfast buffet, available seven days each week, or using the fully equipped kitchen in their own suite. In a hurry? Take along one of the "on-the-go" breakfast bags, also complimentary and available as early as 5:30 A.M. Staybridge Suites hosts a "Sundowner" three evenings a week, with complimentary beer, wine, sodas, and hors d'oeuvres.

Staybridge Suites' "Great Room," used for social activities and dining. Photo by John F. Sanders

Cornhusker Bank occupies a unique position in the Lincoln metro area. In this day of mergers and acquisitions, the bank retains its hometown touch and all the personal services of a true "community bank." Customers have access to all the products and services offered by larger national banks while doing business with a locally owned bank, rich in Lancaster County history.

It all began in 1903 when Farmers State Bank was chartered in Davey, just north of Lincoln. The bank moved to Lincoln in 1960 and became Cornhusker Bank. Today, Cornhusker Bank has six traditional locations throughout the Lincoln area, plus two special branches to serve Lincoln senior citizens at the Legacy and Legacy Terrace Retirement Centers. The bank also provides numerous convenient ATM locations to serve bank customers throughout the city.

The new Cornhusker Bank Technology Center, near the Main Bank at 11th and Cornhusker Highway, provides state-of-the-art data processing services for not only Cornhusker Bank and its customers, but potentially for other banks. Throughout the years, Cornhusker Bank has been known for its technological advances. It was first in Nebraska to initiate CheckImaging, which gives customers a simplified record-keeping system and a copy of each check that clears their account. Today, customers can access their banking information through a variety of ways, including Internet Banking via their home and business computers.

Cornhusker Bank is also known for its commitment to the success of local small businesses. The bank is a premier provider of small business services, including SBA loans, merchant processing for credit card sales, and full-service business insurance. "Business Manager," a newer product, is an accounts receivable purchase program designed to free up cash flow for small businesses. The bank's investment center also assists small business owners by providing retirement plans for their employees.

Evidence of Cornhusker Bank's stability and long service to Lincoln is in the tenure of both its customers and its staff. Bank officers have a service record that averages more than 20 years. Cornhusker Bank remains a family-owned operation. The President/CEO is Lincoln native John F. Dittman. Board Chairman Emeritus Alice Dittman has served the bank for more than 50 years and is well-known around the country for both her knowledge of community banking and her participation in community affairs.

The strengths and dedication of Cornhusker Bank's staff, coupled with the new Technology Center, lead Cornhusker Bank to envision continued growth and expanded services for the citizens of Lincoln and Lancaster County. Whether you own and operate a business or require banking services for your family, Cornhusker Bank remains committed to your success and prepared to serve you. ■

Original bank building in Davey, Nebraska.

F ew Lincoln companies can trace their history farther back than Ameritas. Ameritas was incorporated as the Old Line Bankers Life Insurance Company of Nebraska on April 6, 1887. Organized by five Lincoln businessmen, it was the first local insurance company in Lincoln.

By the 1950s, Bankers Life of Nebraska had grown from a small company serving a limited area of the Midwest to a company with operations from coast to coast. That growth continues today, as Ameritas

Ameritas volunteers assist school children at Pershing Elementary School. Photo by John F. Sanders

provides its customers and policyowners with innovative products and services to help them take control of their financial future.

As a financial services provider, Ameritas is one of the strongest and most respected companies in the industry, offering cutting-edge services and financial strategies for today's business owners and families. The company also is one of the nation's premier providers of group dental insurance.

Ameritas provides both institutional and individual investors a variety of investment vehicles for attaining their financial goals. The company is a national provider of retirement plans for corporate, governmental, and not-for-profit organizations. In addition to providing investment services, Ameritas Investment Corp. is the leading Nebraska-based provider of public financing services, managing municipal bond issues for vital community needs across the state.

AMERITAS
LIFE INSURANCE
CORP.

Ameritas Mutual Insurance Holding Company and Acacia Mutual Holding Corp. formed the first-ever merger between two mutual insurance holding companies on January 1, 1999. This innovative partnership enables Ameritas to offer additional products and services to its customers, including mutual funds and banking.

With ethics and integrity the cornerstones of all its operations, Ameritas Life Insurance Corp. was a national finalist for the Council of Better Business Bureau's "National Torch Award" in 1999—the only company from the insurance/financial business sector to receive this honor.

Ameritas has long supported the Lincoln community with many charitable endeavors, including sponsorship of fine and performing arts and contributions to numerous civic events and organizations. The company participates in the Lincoln Public Schools Ventures in Partnership program with Pershing Elementary School. Ameritas associates continue to be enthusiastic volunteers for a long list of not-for-profit organizations.

As the company embarks on a new millennium (its third century of service), Ameritas and its affiliated divisions and partners continue to lead the way in meeting the financial needs of tomorrow's consumer and business owner.

Ameritas offers the strength, stability, and services you would expect from a national financial services corporation. At the same time, Ameritas provides the personal, caring relationships characteristic of a local company. ■

Ameritas Life Insurance Corp. headquarters in Lincoln. Photo by John F. Sanders

It's fitting that Security Financial Life moved into its new head-quarters at 4000 Pine Lake Road in early 2000. After a solid 105-year record of growth and service to its policyholders, Security Financial Life embarked on exciting new ventures in 1999 and 2000.

First, the company reorganized as a mutual holding company, which dictated a name change from Security Mutual Life to Security Financial Life Insurance Co. (SFL). The new structure provides SFL and its management more flexibility in developing new financial services for customers, and pursuing new growth opportunities as well.

In addition to individual life insurance and annuities, Security Financial Life specializes in providing innovative financial products and services for businesses and profes-sionals, including retirement plans, group insurance, and voluntary employee benefits. The company also has been an industry leader in developing specialty insurance products for businesses, their owners, and employees.

By structuring its marketing efforts into four divisions, the company has focused sales efforts on specific areas of service to customers. A wholly owned subsidiary, Pine Lake Advisors, Inc., was established to implement new approaches to retirement planning, including innovative pension plans for business clients.

The Workplace Products Division has developed a marketing strategy unique to the voluntary employee benefits industry, providing working families an afford-able, payroll-deduction protection package.

The Special Markets Division takes a progressive, innovative approach to developing specialty insurance products tailored to the needs of business owners and their employees.

The Career Agency Division—traditionally the mainspring of Security Financial Life's individual marketing operations—continues to add new general agents to the company's field sales force. SFL is now licensed to operate in 46 states, the District of Columbia, and Guam, carrying the company's product story to individuals and business groups nationwide.

The state-of-the-art building is both highly functional and visually arresting. Photo by John F. Sanders

Perhaps the highlight of the entire company trans-formation was the move into the new headquarters facility in the Pine Lake Road area of south Lincoln, one of the city's fastest growing regions. It is the fifth Lincoln location the company has occupied over the past 105 years.

The new facility utilizes the most current state-of-the-art technology for computer, communication, and energy management capabilities. Both the building and site plans were designed with the flexibility to accommodate a variety of options for future expansion.

Incorporating nearly 60,000 square feet and situated on 7.2 acres, the architecturally distinctive structure features a number of unique design elements in the three-level main building and two-level wing. The spacious lobby and two-story atrium present an inviting "feel" that is carried throughout the building. Large windows afford panoramic views of the Nebraska State Capitol and areas surrounding the building.

With the enhanced resources available through the mutual holding company conversion and completion of its new, state-of-the art facility, Security Financial Life is well positioned for another century of growth and success. ■

The new home office was designed with future growth and expansion in mind. Photo by John F. Sanders

Allied Insurance came to Lincoln in 1965 when the company acquired Standard Reliance Insurance, a small local firm. Today, Allied is a major Lincoln employer with over 400 employees in two locations. The company's new 60,000-square-foot facility in Williamsburg is one of five Allied regional offices.

The company was founded in 1929 in Des Moines, Iowa, as an insurer of private passenger automobiles. Allied still insures motor vehicles,

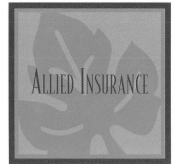

same time reducing costs for both the company and its policyholders.

Allied management focuses on three main objectives, which are the operating tenets of Nationwide Insurance:

• Access. Being accessible to both policyholders and agents.

• Customization. Offering customized products that meet the needs of customers.

• Ease of use. Adapting business procedures to serve the "when and how" needs of each insurance buyer.

Allied recognizes that to meet the needs of customers, it needs to focus on its employees. For that reason, Allied offers one of the best employee training programs in the industry. The training includes career schools, on-the-job training, self-study courses, and continuing education programs. As a company, Allied is committed to offering challenging assignments and opportunities for career growth in order to best serve the insurance buyer of the future.

Allied Insurance is a strong supporter of the Lincoln com-

The company's new 60,000-square-foot facility in Williamsburg is one of five Allied regional offices.

but now the company offers a wide range of personal insurance products and specializes in commercial lines for small to medium size businesses.

Allied is part of the Nationwide Insurance Group, a Fortune 500 company based in Columbus, Ohio. Within the Nationwide Group, Allied is the division that serves independent insurance agents. Allied writes property and casualty insurance in 23 states and expansion plans call for adding other states to the list in the near future.

While Allied's new regional office in Williamsburg serves several north central and southwestern states, the second facility in Lincoln, on North Corner Boulevard, serves as the company-wide Personal Lines Processing Center. More than 200 employees work at each of the Lincoln locations.

Allied has focused on enhancing services to agents and customers through the use of cutting-edge technology. The company's continuing goal is to speed up both the insurance application and claims processing procedures with Internet and online technologies, while at the

munity, both financially and with employee involvement. The company supports numerous community services, including the United Way, Peoples City Mission, the Teammates Mentoring Program, Lincoln Food Bank, and Friendship Home. Allied also participates in Lincoln Public Schools' "Ventures in Partnership" program with Lakeview Elementary School. ■

In-office training sessions allow the company to continually meet its goals. Photo by John F. Sanders

UNICO Group, Inc. is in the insurance and risk management business, but the company is really built on partnerships, says UNICO President Scott Nelson. "Our goal is to partner with our clients, whether businesses or individuals; partner with our employees; and partner with the companies we represent."

The company's mission statement is to provide quality service, professionalism, and excellence to its customers, as well as to improve the quality of life and well being of all employees by allowing for individual creativity, growth, and purpose.

As Lincoln's largest employee-owned property and casualty insurance agency, UNICO Group represents most of the nation's major insurance companies, providing a wide range of options for UNICO clients. "We are unique in many respects, in that we take a creative approach to risk management," Nelson says. "Before we submit an insurance proposal, we sit down with our clients and determine what their major concerns are. Then we propose the programs and steps that we think will best meet each need. It may not always involve an insurance product, but if we can help the client better manage his risks, we have accomplished our mission."

UNICO Group, Inc. has the resources to meet clients' business and personal needs in the area of risk management services, personal and business insurance, self-funding/self-insurance alternatives, fee-based consulting, and bonds. It also serves as a holding company for three subsidiary entities: *UNICO Financial Services, Inc.*, which develops group employee benefit programs, including group health, retirement plans, Section 125 cafeteria plans, group short-term and long-term disability insurance, and group life insurance for companies;

UNICO Financial Advisors, Inc., which provides individual life, disability income, long-term care, and voluntary group programs; and *UNICO Group of Columbus, Inc.*, a full-line agency serving the out-of-state interests of Nebraska.

UNICO markets its products and services throughout Nebraska, as well as providing insurance programs to clients who have operations around the country. In the Lincoln area, UNICO is a major provider of insurance and benefit programs to the

Management Team, left to right: Sandra Masters, Scott Nelson, and Bob Reynoldson. Photo by John F. Sanders

medical community, the construction industry, and major financial institutions. UNICO also works with association programs, local educational groups, and provides insurance programs to governmental entities at both state and local levels.

UNICO was formed in 1988, but its roots go back to the past century. O.W. Palm started a Lincoln insurance agency in 1892, which eventually became Reynolds-Simmons-Nelson. Meanwhile, Chambers-Dobson Financial Services was formed by Jess Chambers and Robert Dobson in 1941. The two agencies merged in 1988 and moved to 4435 O Street in the UNICO Building.

Along with its wide-ranging risk management services to clients, UNICO is known for its commitment to the Lincoln community. Nearly every staff member is involved in one or more community service activities. UNICO employees traditionally participate in a special community project every fall.

UNICO's future plans are to continue to partner with its clients, its employees, and its companies, to empower them and continue the winning spirit. ■

Account Executives, top row, left to right: Sharon Bair, Joe Blahak, Mike Meyer, Bob Reynoldson, Scott Nelson, and Ed Packard. Bottom Row, left to right: Andy Drake, Rich Hill, Kent Sprague, Scott Bowhay, and Mike Herring. Photo by John F. Sanders

W hile the past decade has seen considerable upheaval in the financial services industry, Union Bank has tripled in asset size and more than doubled the number of its employees since 1990. It's all in keeping with Union Bank's commitment to three fundamental beliefs:

• Excellent customer service that is second to none and surpasses customer expectations.

• Employee satisfaction in an open environment that fosters trust and loyalty, and where employees have an opportunity to excel.

• Diversified financial services and products to provide a broad base of services for customer needs.

affiliated companies is UNIPAC, one of the largest organizations in the country servicing Guaranteed Student Loans.

Union Bank was the first Nebraska-based commercial bank to develop and manage its own family of mutual funds. The Stratus Funds Family was established in 1991 and now includes four funds, with Union Bank serving as investment advisor. The bank also created InvestStar, an investment service for customers that offers stocks, bonds, mutual funds, annuities, and tax-advantaged investments.

Outside of "working hours," Union Bank staff members support many civic, charitable, and community organizations by donating both time and money. Corporately, Union Bank has established a share of annual earnings for contributions back into the community, specifically for education, the arts, and community betterment.

As a new decade begins, Union Bank continues to expand its specialized services to customers. The bank now serves more than 65,000 Nebraska households and businesses. The former First National Bank Lincoln was merged into Union Bank in 1998, the same year Union Bank's new landmark office building was opened at 27th and Pine Lake Road.

Buildings and locations are secondary, however, to the overall Union Bank goal of providing delivery systems of choice for its customers. Whether your choice is a regular bank lobby, grocery store branch bank, telephone, ATM, or computer—Union Bank is making banking easy. Through all these means, Union Bank offers products, services, and information to help customers meet their goals and achieve their dreams. ◼

In 1956, this building was constructed at 48th and Bancroft. From one location in College View, the bank has expanded to 30 across the state and developed into a financially diverse organization. Photo by John F. Sanders

It began in 1917 as Farmers State Bank, headquartered at 48th and Prescott in College View. The name was changed to Union Bank in 1935 and, when trust powers were added to the bank's services in 1959, it became Union Bank & Trust Company. In 1965, the Dunlap family, long-time Nebraska bankers, purchased Union Bank & Trust.

Today, Union Bank has 30 offices throughout the eastern two-thirds of Nebraska, including 13 locations in Lincoln. The bank serves several niche markets, including its role as Nebraska's largest Small Business Administration lender and the second largest bank lender to agriculture. The bank also is the top mortgage lender in Lincoln.

Union Bank is Nebraska's largest student loan lender and among the top 10 in the nation. The bank manages student loan origination programs in 37 states. One of Union Bank's eight

The office at 6801 South 27th Street (27th and Pine Lake Road) is home to the trust division, including traditional trust, investments, and retirement plans, as well as retail and lending services. Photo by John F. Sanders

Architects design the structures; M.E. Group engineers bring the structures to life. That, in essence, is what M.E. Group is all about—the inner workings and operation of modern-day buildings.

Since 1982, the staff of M.E. Group has provided engineering services for mechanical, electrical, plumbing, temperature control, and life safety systems for new and renovated buildings. The firm's services often include consulting on cable design for telecommunications, indoor and outdoor lighting, fire and security systems, chilled water systems, power distribution, and central plant design and commissioning.

Lincoln is home base for M.E. Group, with regional offices in Omaha, Kansas City, Denver, and Des Moines to provide closer coordination and on-site contact with builders and contractors in those areas. The company began as Maniktala Engineering Group with a handful of engineers. It became M.E. Group in 1992, and now has a staff of more than 50 employees. Company principals have worked together an average 23 years.

M.E. Group engineers offer services ranging from preliminary studies to complete turnkey jobs. The company has worked on projects ranging from less than $10,000 to over $200,000,000 in construction costs. Recent M.E. Group projects include the new Gallop World Headquarters in Omaha and several new buildings in South Lincoln's Williamsburg development.

M.E. Group's project list ranges the entire gamut of the alphabet, from airports to zoos. The company has engineered several projects for Kansas City International Airport, including a major terminal building renovation;

handled projects for the new Denver International Airport, including a 2,200-car parking structure; and designed projects for both the Lincoln Airport Authority and Duncan Aviation. M.E. Group is a leader in green, sustainable, energy, and environmental designs.

M.E. Group was instrumental in designing a new entry building for the Kansas City Zoo. Criteria for the project included state-of-the-art energy efficiency and environmentally friendly materials. M.E. Group also participated in a $26 million improvement project for Truman Medical Center in Kansas City and furnished mechanical and electrical design for over 20 golf course clubhouses, including two in the San Francisco Bay area.

Recent industrial projects have included Garner Industries, Linweld, Addax, Lincoln Plating, Lincoln Composites, and Goodyear. Commercial and office complexes and campuses include First Data Resources, Hewlett Packard, Enron, Empire Fire and Marine, and Farm Bureau Insurance.

M.E. Group has a strong employee and family orientation. Several staff members are stockholders. "Our families come first, then our work," says founder and principal Ravi Maniktala. "Our goal is to add value to every person we touch—employee, associate, or client. Likewise, we aim to add value to the communities in which we work."

Most M.E. Group staff members are active in one or more service organizations, and Maniktala has served with such groups as Rotary, the Lincoln Public Schools Foundation, and advisory committees for the UNL College of Engineering. *For more information please visit www.megroup.com.* ■

Varieties in project size and type provide challenges and enjoyment in meeting client needs.

Imagine…it's a sunny fall afternoon in Lincoln, 12:30, and kick-off is coming up for another Cornhusker football game. In another part of Lincoln, though, a Talent+ associate is conducting a telephone interview with a young lady in Thailand. She's a candidate for the sales manager's job at a new hotel in Hong Kong.

This example highlights the services offered to corporations and organizations around the world by Talent+, based right here in Lincoln.

Talent+ is an international human resource consulting firm that provides companies of all sizes—from Fortune 50 to start-up growth firms—customized solutions in recruitment, selection, and development of their personnel. The company developed the proprietary assessment tool, known as the Talent+ Quality Selection Process^{SM} (QSP), in order to identify individual talents, strengths, potential and aptitude for specific jobs. The QSP is an integrated program that guides human resource staffs through the entire hiring process, from initial interview through selection and hiring.

Benefits to client organizations may include increased profits, enhanced sales productivity, and greater customer satisfaction. Firms using the process often have lower employee turnover and fewer customer complaints.

Talent+ clients include retail apparel chain Ann Taylor, The Ritz-Carlton Hotel Company, Nordstrom, Pepperidge Farm, Godiva Chocolatier, the Mayo Clinic, and many other well-known organizations.

Since its founding in 1989, Talent+ has grown at an average rate of 30 percent a year, with 99 percent of the company's new business coming from referrals.

Along with revenues, the company's workplace has grown rapidly, too. Talent+ today has more than 100 associates, 80 percent of whom are based in Lincoln.

Talent+ conducts telephone interviews in more than 20 languages and does interviews 24 hours a day, seven days a week, to accommodate time zone differences around the globe. The company maintains a close working relationship with both the language department and statistics experts at the University of Nebraska-Lincoln.

Talent+ began operations with just five individuals. Doug Rath and the late Dr. William E. Hall, UNL psychology professor, founded the company, and were soon joined by Doug's wife, Kimberly K. Rath, Sandra Maxwell, and Susan Hall, wife of Dr. Hall. Both Doug and Kimberly studied under Dr. Hall's Nebraska Human Resources Institute at UNL.

Dr. Hall taught that everyone has talent. The key is placing that talent in the right position for a successful career. That basic concept continues to guide the operations of Talent+ as the company continues to grow and expand.

Many Talent+ associates are involved in community betterment activities in addition to their workday specialties. The company has sponsored numerous community service projects, including $10,000 to the "Can Caravan," and made contributions to dozens of human service projects in Lincoln. In fact, Talent+ has received several awards for being the number one worksite for employer support of the Community Services Fund campaign for five consecutive years.

Talent+ celebrates its associates and their families in many ways. One of their annual events is the 4th of July celebration. Associates, their families, and friends gather for an evening of good food, fun, and spectacular fireworks. ■

Talent+ today has more than 100 associates, 80 percent of whom are based in Lincoln. Photo by John F. Sanders

Talent+ celebrates the 4th of July with associates, their families, and friends. Photo by Patty Geist

Photo by Pat McDonogh

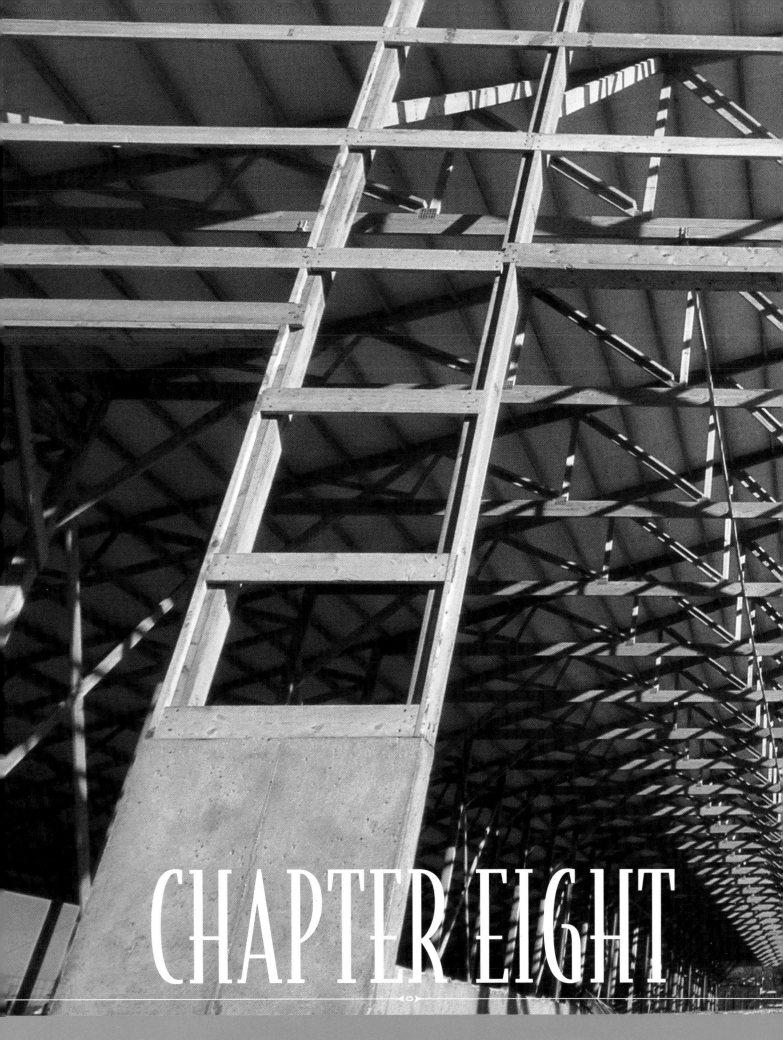

CHAPTER EIGHT

Real Estate, Development & Construction

I t all started with a $400 invest-
ment and five sales associates.
Today, it has grown into the largest
real estate firm serving Lincoln and
the surrounding communities. That's
the story of HOME Real Estate.

Now a multimillion-dollar
operation, with approximately
300 individual Realtors® serving
homebuyers and sellers, HOME
Real Estate has been a vital part of
Lincoln's growth. As the pace of city expansion has
picked up, HOME Real Estate has increased its presence
in the marketplace.

HOME Real Estate is the leader in new construction
home sales, representing more than 50 of Lincoln's finest
homebuilders. The company has been involved with
over 50 subdivisions citywide, and continues to play a
major role in new developments in and around Lincoln.

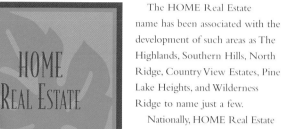

The HOME Real Estate
name has been associated with the
development of such areas as The
Highlands, Southern Hills, North
Ridge, Country View Estates, Pine
Lake Heights, and Wilderness
Ridge to name just a few.

Nationally, HOME Real Estate
ranks 92nd among the country's 500
largest real estate brokers and 47th
among the largest privately owned
independent real estate firms. This puts the company at
the forefront of Nebraska area real estate firms.

HOME Real Estate has taken a proactive approach
to the integration of technology in the real estate
business, and provides its sales force with the best
technological tools and education available. Both
Realtors® and clients have access to current properties
and information through the company's web site at
www.homerealestate.com. As technology
advances, HOME Real Estate intends to
stay on the leading edge of innovation in
serving its customers.

The HOME Real Estate story actually
began in 1938 when Henry Austin joined a
local firm. Two years later, he took over the
firm and, with his wife Edith, embarked on
a lifelong career in the real estate business.
Initially, the company had one office and
five sales associates. Their primary business
was property management.

After Henry Austin passed away in 1948,
Edith sold part of the business and moved
the firm to 3910 South Street in 1955.

The location of Austin Realty at 3910 South Street beginning in 1955.

The 3910 South Street location as it appears today. It is now one of six HOME Real Estate sales offices in Lincoln. Photo by John F. Sanders

She was responsible for redirecting the company's business emphasis toward real estate sales. Edith sold Austin Realty to Gerald Schleich and another partner in 1964, and Schleich became sole owner one year later. The company was renamed HOME Real Estate in 1988. HOME Real Estate remains a family oriented company and Gerald Schleich's sons carry on active management of the organization today.

Throughout his career, Gerald Schleich has had a positive influence on the real estate industry in Nebraska, at the local, state, and national level. He has served as president of the Lincoln Board of Realtors® and the Nebraska Realtors® Association, and has served as a director of the National Association of Realtors®. He was appointed to the 10th District Economic Advisory Council of the Federal Reserve Bank of Kansas City in 1995.

That commitment to service and community has carried over to the entire HOME Real Estate staff. Several HOME brokers and sales associates are past presidents of both the Lincoln Board of Realtors® and the Nebraska Realtors® Association. The HOME Real Estate staff has dedicated countless hours to both associations as officers, committee chairpersons, and volunteers.

Company staff and associates have donated both time and funds to many community groups and activities over the years, including the Asian Cultural Center, Bright Lights, Cedars Home for Children, Folsom Children's Zoo, Friends of Lied, Hispanic Community Center, Lincoln Arts Council, Nebraska Special Olympics, Peoples City Mission, and hundreds of other organizations. HOME Real Estate has been actively involved in Lincoln Public Schools'Ventures in Partnership Program and won the 1999 Pioneer Award for the company's efforts on behalf of Hartley Elementary School.

Moving into a new century and the new millennium, HOME Real Estate continues to focus on excellence in service, to its clients and to the community. The company continues to reach out with new innovations and even better ways to serve Lincoln and its citizens. At the same time, HOME continues to provide a strong path of growth and prosperity for its own associates and for those with whom they interact in various ways.

HOME Real Estate now serves the Lincoln community from six primary offices and offers clients complete real estate services, including lot sales, new construction sales, in-house lending, and title insurance services. In addition, through its association with national real estate networks, HOME Real Estate can offer top quality real estate services anywhere in North America.

The company's guiding principle for the future remains: "Lincoln—a great place to call HOME." ■

HOME Real Estate's newest sales office, located at 5901 North 27th Street, was built in 2000. Photo by John F. Sanders

HOME Real Estate's Pine Lake office was built in 1998 at 7211 South 27th Street. Photo by John F. Sanders

Woods Bros. Realty's guiding principle is "we are not selling just houses; we are selling lifestyles," says Woods Bros. President F. Pace Woods Jr. And Woods Bros. has been doing just that since 1889. Block by block, lot by lot, Woods Bros. has been instrumental in building the Lincoln we know today.

With nearly 300 sales associates, Woods Bros. Realty handles nearly half the real estate sales in the company's market area and participates in two-thirds of all real estate sales.

WOODS BROS. REALTY

roof. These additional services are designed to provide the utmost in convenience for real estate buyers and sellers.

"Even though Woods Bros. is an 'old' company, we are continually developing new ideas and considering new concepts," says Pace Woods. Not surprising, he says. The company's predecessors have all been progressive, innovative leaders.

Frederick Woods first came to Lincoln in 1876, after developing real estate for Marshall Field in Downers Grove, Illinois, near Chicago. He later became a prominent livestock auctioneer and acquired the title of "Colonel Woods." He and his wife, Eliza, raised four sons and two daughters, Fannie and Helen.

Frederick's four sons, Frank, Mark, Albert, and George, all achieved success in various ways. Mark, for example, shot upland birds and doves as a teenager for Lincoln's hotel dining rooms. At age 19, he took a train to Montana territory to buy cattle from Indian tribes. Before the tribal representatives would parlay, Mark had to wrestle the strongest brave in the tribe. He won. The Indians didn't realize he was captain of the University of Nebraska's wrestling team.

He returned to Lincoln with the cattle, fattened them in the Burlington feedlots where Pioneers Park is now located, and made his first million dollars. Years later, Mark was instrumental in getting the railroad to donate the abandoned feedlots to the city for the development of Pioneers Park. The Burlington's president even commissioned the bison sculpture that marks the park entrance today.

Woods Bros. Agent Services and Corporate headquarters. Photo by John F. Sanders

"Our sales associates sell more properties per agent, on average, than those from any other firm," says Woods. It is this kind of expertise and experience that earns Woods Bros. number one ranking in service, based on independent public surveys.

"We are a traditional company filled with young, energetic, innovative people who strive to do the best job for customers they can possibly do," Woods says.

Woods Bros. Realty works with some of the most prominent and award-winning builders in the area. The company currently is developing its 74th residential addition to Lincoln, and has exclusive marketing arrangements with other leading developments such as Williamsburg, HiMark Golf Course, Vintage Heights, Rolling Hills, The Ridge, and Fallbrook.

Woods Bros. Realty has grown along with Lincoln. The company has five Lincoln offices, plus brokerage offices in Seward, Beatrice, and Grand Island. Woods Bros. also has introduced new concepts in real estate sales and service. The company was the first to offer sales associates the opportunity to work under a 100 percent commission plan, or a conventional graduated scale plan.

Always on the cutting edge with new ideas and technologies, Woods Bros. is the only company in Southeast Nebraska that offers "one stop shopping" real estate services. The firm's "partnership" companies include Capitol Title and Escrow, Community Mortgage, Woods Bros. Insurance, and Community Land Surveying, all of which are located under one

Woods Bros. first headquarters still stands on South 13th Street.

Owners and managers of Woods Bros. and partner companies. Photo by John F. Sanders

Mark Woods developed his first residential subdivision, Hillsdale, in 1886 in the 20th and A Street area. The Woods brothers used this area as a springboard for further developments to the south, west, and east. Mark's son, Pace Woods, Sr., drove a buckboard down the ridge line with Mark and his brother George putting American flags on either side to mark the 100 foot right of way for Sheridan Boulevard.

After further developing the Woodscrest and South 24th Street areas, Mark arranged for the Country Club of Lincoln to be moved from the vicinity of Gooch Mills to its present location. This was done to bring additional development over the hill south of Van Dorn Street.

The Woods family was instrumental in the development of Pioneers Park. Photo by John F. Sanders

Following World War I, Mark and George manufactured motor trucks in a factory in north Lincoln. The trucks were named "The Patriot" after General John J. Pershing, a close friend of the Woods. Pace Sr. took over the factory in the 1920s and manufactured the Arrow Sport biplane, one of which hangs at Lincoln's municipal airport. At the time, the factory had the largest straight-line airplane production line in the world, turning out five planes a week. That building is now Lincoln's Goodyear Plant.

The Woods family continued their operations in real estate and developed tracts in part of Havelock, through the UNL East Campus area, on to the south and southeast. From A Street South, between 17th and 48th Streets, much of Lincoln was platted and developed by Woods Bros.

F. Pace Woods Jr. returned to Lincoln in 1959, after spending 10 years in Hollywood with the ABC and NBC television networks. He headed up advertising and promotion for NBC's flagship station KNBH, and later was a TV director for Dinah Shore, Jimmy Durante, Bob Hope, and other celebrities.

Intending to stay for six months, he instead took over management of Woods Bros. Realty and remains in that capacity today. Company ownership, originally limited to family members, has been broadened to include members of the management team.

"Ownership enhances commitment, which translates into the highest level of service to our clients, our staff, and our sales associates," Woods says. "Six generations of Lincoln and Southeast Nebraska families have made Woods Bros. Realty a real estate leader. More than half our business is repeat business. We intend to continue that tradition." ∎

Ayars & Ayars, Inc. began operations with three employees and the goal of becoming a leading design/build general contractor. That was 1985, when the design/build concept was still a new idea.

Today, Ayars & Ayars is 130 members strong, with four offices in Lincoln, Omaha, York, and Des Moines. The company provides architectural services, project management, steel erection, masonry installation, concrete work, gypsum installation, and carpentry. The firm's client list reads like a "Who's Who" of national companies, and the company has become a leader in the design/build delivery process in the region.

This 2,348-cubic-yard concrete pour was completed in just 12 hours as part of a new wastewater treatment plant. Pre-planning and on-site coordination were key to pulling off a feat that the engineers said couldn't be done.

Design/build is a cooperative concept in which the architect and contractor work together with the owner to design a project that allows for most efficient use of resources. The process helps save both time and construction costs. The design/build concept seeks to avoid adversarial situations which too often occur when a project starts with the architect's design and the contractor comes into the picture much later.

Ayars & Ayars has expanded the design/build concept even further to incorporate partnering relationships with suppliers and subcontractors during the design and construction phases. This allows for utilization of each partner's expertise to deliver the best possible building solution for the project.

At Ayars & Ayars, this process is called "Ayars Quality Leadership" (AQL), the Ayars & Ayars version of Total Quality Management (TQM). AQL incorporates guidelines for continuous improvement of each project, starting with the initial sales contact and continuing through design, construction, accounting, right through to the last person to walk off the jobsite. AQL builds teamwork throughout the process, focusing on the needs and expectations of the client.

Although based in the heartland, the company's reach extends far beyond the Midwest. Ayars & Ayars has completed projects across the United States, including large pharmaceutical warehouses in New

York and Puerto Rico and prison dormitories for the Texas Department of Criminal Justice.

Ayars & Ayars has completed over 1,000 projects in 11 states and Puerto Rico, ranging in size from small office remodels to a large distribution center covering 425,000 square feet. Ayars & Ayars clients include: Kawasaki, DuPont, Sharp Electronics, Goodyear Tire & Rubber Company, Burlington Northern Railroad, Pfizer Animal Health, Firestone, Duncan Aviation, Blockbuster Video, Harley Davidson, Square D, University of Nebraska, Excel Corporation, IBP, Monsanto/Solaris Group, Taco Johns, Subway Sandwich Shops, Speedway Motors, and the Indianapolis Colts.

Local projects include the Lincoln Stars hockey facility, Linweld distribution facilities, First Federal Bank, General Excavating office, Isco offices and manufacturing spaces, Lincoln Airport Authority offices and hangars, and the Nebraska Lottery offices. Several Ayars & Ayars projects have been recognized with awards from the American Concrete Institute and the Associated Builders and Contractors.

Construction awards are not the only area in which the Ayars & Ayars team has been a winner. Safety awards have recognized the company's emphasis on safety. By its very nature, construction can be hazardous work. For this reason, safety is a high priority in the Ayars Quality Leadership Program.

Ayars & Ayars has received awards from both the Nebraska Safety Council and the Iowa Safety Council for the company's leadership in developing safety programs, safety training, and job safety. Safety training in the Ayars & Ayars program includes First Aid, CPR, fall protection, equipment operation, back safety training, drug and alcohol awareness, and asbestos awareness.

The Ayars steel crews tread carefully high above the ground. Safety is the number one focus in day-to-day operations for Ayars & Ayars, Inc.

"The safety of our people and all those involved with our projects is more important than the concrete, wood, and steel that they work with," says Ayars & Ayars President Mike Ayars. "All our employees participate in safety meetings, and safety reminders are kept highly visible throughout the company, including both in the offices and out on the jobsites."

Worker cross-training is another unique feature of the AQL program. Metals crews learn concrete work, carpenters learn metals work, masons learn carpentry, and so on. This cross-training enables employees to enhance their skill levels and knowledge of the construction process, as well as allowing for more efficient crew scheduling at times of greater need on a project. The emphasis on cross training ties in with the company's goal of continuous improvement.

Many Lincoln community projects have benefited from the skills of Ayars & Ayars staff members. The company has been an active supporter of the YWCA's Project Youth, helping raise funds for summer camps and day-care services. Cedars Home for Children and the Lincoln Rape/Spouse Abuse Crisis Center have received support from Ayars & Ayars employees. Company staff have volunteered time and expertise to improve the athletic fields at Lincoln Northeast High School.

Four Ayars & Ayars staff are members of the Urban Search and Rescue Group, Nebraska Task Force 1, which specializes in rigging and lifting operations. These volunteers were called to duty in the aftermath of Hurricane Opal and for a grain elevator explosion in Kansas. Ayars & Ayars received special recognition from the city of Lincoln for the company's help in clean-up efforts after the paralyzing blizzard of October 1997. Ayars & Ayars volunteers spent hundreds of hours and operated the company's heavy equipment in support of city workcrews.

Once a horse-show arena at the Nebraska State fair grounds, the Ayars team completed renovations to this building, transforming it into "The Ice Box," home of the USHL Lincoln Stars.

"Ayars & Ayars has been fortunate to participate in Lincoln's rapid growth these past 10 years," says Mike Ayars. "We look forward to continued growth in this new millennium, and will continue to deliver the highest quality in construction projects for the Lincoln area. We also will continue to value the importance of family when scheduling our commitments, so that Ayars & Ayars workers also can enjoy the benefits of living in the Lincoln community.

"We believe in Lincoln's future, and will continue to contribute to that future." ◼

I f you have visited one of Lincoln's newest and most distinctive areas, Williamsburg Village, you have seen the work of Hampton Enterprises, Inc. and its wholly owned subsidiary, Hampton Commercial Construction, Inc.

The distinctive colonial design and architectural detail in both the commercial buildings and the residential areas of Williamsburg Village are visible evidence of the pride of craftsmanship that goes into Hampton Enterprises' projects. "We wanted to create a unique environment here in Lincoln that ranks with the best architectural examples in the country," says Mark Bronder, Hampton Enterprises President and CEO. Bronder is the second-generation representative of the family owned business.

Hampton Enterprises officially came into being in 1964, but its roots go back nearly 30 years before that. America and Nebraska were in the throes of the Great Depression. Determined to better his lot, Joe Hampton entered Chadron State College after graduation from high school. When his funds ran out after just one semester, Joe became an apprentice electrician, working for 70¢ an hour.

Hampton moved to Lincoln in 1947 because he could get 20¢ an hour more here. He was 22 years old and had $40 in capital. He began building a house in his spare time, evenings, and weekends, intending it to be his own home. However, housing was short in postwar Lincoln and he sold his new house for

$9,800 even before it was finished. So he built another, then another. It was the beginning of a pioneering enterprise that set the pace for development in the Lincoln area.

Joe Hampton made the giant step from homebuilder to developer in 1964 when he purchased 80 acres of ground at 70th and A Streets for $160,000. He paid half the purchase price in cash. That first venture became the area now known as Lincolnshire Square, one of the first combination office parks and residential community developments in Lincoln.

Shown are two properties owned, leased, managed, and constructed by Hampton Enterprises, Inc. This 42,000-square-foot multi-tenant office building is located in the firm's Corporate Centre Office Park development. Photo by John F. Sanders

Meanwhile, Hampton Enterprises and Hampton Commercial Construction have grown, now employing more than 50 people in a vertically integrated enterprise. The companies are engaged in land development, real estate services, general contracting, construction

Located in Williamsburg Village, this 60,000-square-foot office building is occupied by Allied Insurance, a Nationwide Insurance Company.

Completed for Lincoln Public Schools, Hunnigton Elementary contains 72,000 square feet and a 525-student capacity. Photo by John F. Sanders

management, and property management including building maintenance, lawn and landscaping services, tree relocation, and snow removal.

Hampton Commercial Construction, the general contracting and construction management division of the company, provides construction services for many project types. "We utilize the newest advances in construction technology," says Mark Bronder. "That, plus our responsive attitude and adherence to our founder's philosophy of building excellence are the primary reasons for our success. The repeat business we continue to receive from major clients confirms our efforts."

As a general contractor, Hampton Commercial Construction encourages partnering concepts in its projects. "We believe a close working relationship with the owner and the other members of the construction team is crucial to project success," Bronder adds.

Major Developments

Hampton Enterprises has developed several distinctive residential subdivisions, in addition to Williamsburg Village and Lincolnshire. Southfork Estates and Lancashire Estates are examples of other Hampton projects. Other commercial projects include Corporate Centre Office Park and Meadowlane Shopping Center.

Hampton Enterprises began Williamsburg with the purchase of 320 acres in 1989. As Lincoln's first master-planned community, the area offers a prestige location for many businesses, as well as providing an award-winning, self-contained community with residential, workplace, and shopping amenities. Hampton Commercial Construction has done the major part of the contracting work in the development. "We purposely instituted strict design covenants to ensure that all building designs follow the colonial style and meet high standards of construction and architectural quality," says Mark Bronder.

Although it was started more than 20 years ago, Lincolnshire Square Office Park is still undergoing development today. Along with attractive residential areas, there are 20 office buildings within the area and more are on the drawing board, including a major four-story complex with up to 50,000 square feet of space.

Another Hampton Enterprises development is Corporate Centre Office Park at 75th and O Streets. Started in 1990, Corporate Centre already has six structures in place, four of which have been sold to other companies. The major building to date is a four-story office building with 42,000 square feet and housing some 15 tenants, many of which are medical offices. Another 85,000 square feet of commercial office space remains to be constructed.

"Our company structure of integrated specialties allows us to better control quality of our projects, as well as scheduling and delivery," says Bronder. "It is also our corporate philosophy to 'self-perform' construction and renovation work, and follow up with our own maintenance and management programs. We can control costs better, and maintain higher quality in all stages."

"Day-to-day business activities within Hampton Enterprises, Inc. and Hampton Commercial Construction, Inc. are guided by our core values of honesty and integrity, quality, commitment, employee welfare, and community involvement," says Mark Bronder. "We are firmly committed to providing a safe and creative workplace for our people and promoting a genuine concern for the well-being of our employee families."

Hampton employees are active in a long list of charitable organizations and community activities. Joe Hampton set the example years ago with his own involvement in community affairs, including serving 14 years on the Lincoln Airport Authority Board and 12 years on the Lincoln City Council. "We are always looking for ways to make our community a better place in which to live and work," Bronder says. ■

Douglas Theatre Company proudly presents South Pointe Cinema, a six-screen, stadium-style seating movie theatre completed by Hampton. Photo by John F. Sanders

For nearly a century the companies that trace their roots to Abel Construction Company have been building Lincoln and Nebraska.

George Abel, Sr., graduated from the University of Nebraska with a civil engineering degree in 1906. Although he went to work for the Chicago, Burlington & Quincy Railroad, he had a goal of starting his own business.

With savings of $100, he started Abel Construction Company in 1908. His first equipment purchases: Six heavy shovels, two steel wheelbarrows, and one hand concrete mixer. His first jobs included installing a

Company was renamed NEBCO, Inc. the same year. Today, the companies are third-generation family owned and operated business with more than 900 employees. NEBCO's operations span the entire state of Nebraska, supplying the construction industry with the materials to construct buildings, streets, and highways. Other NEBCO business interests include mining, finance, real estate development, agriculture, transportation, railroading, warehousing, insurance, and surety bonding.

Concrete Industries, Inc., a NEBCO subsidiary, is one of the region's premier suppliers of high-quality precast/prestressed concrete building and bridge systems and reinforced concrete pipe. Operations include state-of-the-art manufacturing facilities, a fleet of delivery trucks, and erection services.

NEBCO also manufactures and distributes concrete block and concrete brick to the construction trades. NEBCO founded General Testing Laboratory in 1961 to provide a higher level of quality control for the concrete products made by the company. GTL conducts on-site inspections of all precast concrete products produced each and every day.

As the use of concrete in paving became more widespread, George Abel, Sr. founded the Ready Mixed Concrete Company. One of the first permanent ready mixed concrete plants in the nation was built at 18th and Y Streets in Lincoln. Ready mixed concrete was mixed in three-cubic-yard loads and delivered from the plant in dump trucks to Lincoln construction sites.

The plant at 18th and Y was remodeled several times and finished as a completely new plant in 1993. Today, ready mixed concrete is produced at the company's eight plants in southeast and central Nebraska, and supplied to job sites by a fleet of more than 100 transit mixer trucks. Trucks are leased by the company's operating divisions from the NEBCO Fleet Garage. Three Lincoln locations provide service and maintenance for over 225 vehicles,

Ready Mixed plant at 18th and Y (1944).

concrete floor in a local laundry facility and building a concrete bridge and driveway for a private residence.

As the 20th century progressed, significant transportation changes were occurring. Dirt roads gave way to paved streets. The automobile replaced the horse and buggy. State highways were paved, and were superceded by the new interstate highway system.

During the early years, Abel Construction Company was heavily involved in municipal and highway concrete and asphalt paving. The company also expanded into other enterprises, such as ready-mixed concrete, concrete pipe, fabrication of steel reinforcing bars, railroading, warehousing, and even farming. Abel Investment Company was established in 1949 as a material supply and investment organization, separate from the construction company.

Abel Construction Company became Constructors, Inc. in 1974. Abel Investment

Ready Mixed plant at 18th and Y today.

including automobiles, pickups, boom and dump trucks, transit mixers, tractors, flatbed trailers, and tankers.

George P. Abel, Jr. took over the helm of the family business in 1945 and succeeded his mother, Hazel Hempel Abel, as president in 1951. He graduated from UNL with a degree in business administration in 1942. He competed with the university's track team for three years and played guard and halfback for the Cornhusker football team. He played in the Rose Bowl game against Stanford January 1, 1941. Following graduation, he served in the U.S. Army during World War II.

George P. Abel, Jr. and his four sisters founded another NEBCO subsidiary, Universal Surety Company, in 1947. The company writes contract surety bonds that pledge the surety's credit to insure that a contractor successfully completes projects and pays all bills. Universal Surety Company is Nebraska's largest writer of surety bonds. A sister company, Inland Insurance Company, was founded in 1958 to handle similar functions. Over time, both

companies expanded their services to include license and permit bonds, public, official, and court bonds, and miscellaneous bonds such as probate and guardianship bonds. Both companies are licensed to do business in 20 states.

James P. Abel succeeded his father, George Abel, Jr., as president of NEBCO, Inc. in 1985. The company has continued its growth in concrete and building materials production and has branched out into commercial and recreational real estate development. NEBCO has developed Class A office properties along Lincoln Mall near the State Capitol and at Chalco Valley Business Park at the southwestern edge of Omaha.

Under Jim's leadership, the company developed Quarry Oaks Golf Club near Mahoney State Park and is currently embarking on a bold new commercial/ residential project in northwest Lincoln, called Fallbrook. The 600-acre development will include an office park, residential areas, a school, shops, parks, and trails, all with convenient access to major highways including I-80.

One of NEBCO's most visible new projects is Haymarket Park at 6th and Charleston Streets in Lincoln. NEBCO is participating in this major development with the City of Lincoln and the University of Nebraska. The stadium opened June 1, 2001, and is home to the Lincoln Saltdogs, a new minor league baseball team owned by NEBCO.

NEBCO continues to grow with Lincoln and Nebraska. ■

The Platte River provides a scenic backdrop to several greens on the Quarry Oaks golf course.

Lincoln Saltdogs baseball Haymarket Park. Photo by Richard Voges, Lincoln, Nebraska

Many of Lincoln's newest developments have a unique "feel" because of a layout that includes housing, service facilities and commercial buildings within the same area. The idea is to make such areas more conducive to families, so that they can live, work and play in the same area. Attractive commons areas with mature trees, landscaping, bike paths, etc. separate residential areas and commercial areas. But the "mixed use" layout makes the entire neighborhood more convenient for working families.

HAMPTON DEVELOPMENT SERVICES, INC.

Both Stone Bridge Creek and North Creek, like all HDS neighborhoods, will include plenty of green spaces and common areas, including bike and walking paths that lead to area restaurants and the future new elementary and high schools.

With an eye to focusing more on land development, Bob Hampton left the family business in 1994 to concentrate on his own projects. He grew up in the construction business, mowing lawns, framing houses, pouring concrete, and learning all the other jobs that go into the construction business. Eventually, he moved into management with Hampton Enterprises, but decided land and project development was more to his liking.

Today, Hampton Development Services has a relatively small team of development specialists. HDS lays out new development sites, such as Stone Bridge Creek and North Creek, then works closely with subcontractors to do the initial site preparation. Once plans are approved and site grading, streets, and utilities are done, HDS generally sells the lots to future homeowners and contractors.

"We also develop properties for our own portfolio," says Bob Hampton. "Occasionally, we will build the commercial part of a new development and lease and manage it ourselves. Or, we may sell part and retain ownership of part of the project."

HDS works with many of Lincoln's best-known builders and contractors in developing projects. "Once we develop a site, we may work with contractors who specialize in apartments, retirement, retail, or flex office space," Hampton says.

While at Hampton Enterprises, Bob was active in the development of Williamsburg Village, Lancashire Estates, and Southfork Estates. HDS is the developer of Vintage Heights at 84th and Old Cheney Road.

Williamsburg Village entry way. Photo by John F. Sanders

Prime examples are the existing Williamsburg Village at 40th and Old Cheney, and now Stone Bridge Creek on the north side of the Interstate 80 and North 27th Street interchange, and North Creek on the south side of the same interchange. Bob Hampton and his Hampton Development Services team are developing these new areas. The new developments cover 600 acres and will eventually include homes and apartments, retirement housing, churches, retail areas, office facilities, warehouse sites, daycare facilities and "flex" buildings. Hundreds of high quality jobs are located in the area, including Centurion's new corporate headquarters and manufacturing operation. Cabela's new telephone facility is nearby. So is the Kawasaki plant, which recently announced another major expansion. The UNL Technology Park is close by, along with other major employers in the Highlands and Air Park West.

"The idea is that residents can live, work, and play in one of Lincoln's finest neighborhoods and business parks," says Bob Hampton. "Residents can live close to where they work, reducing the stress and time loss of commuting. Many of the local services can be reached by walking or biking, cutting down on automobile use."

Site of Centurion Wireless Technology's new home in Stone Bridge Creek at 27th and I-80. Photo by John F. Sanders

The Vintage Heights development spans some 420 acres, most of which is residential. A neighborhood retail center is planned at the southeast corner of 84th and Old Cheney Road, and new public elementary and middle schools will be nearby. A daycare center and Catholic church and school are part of the development plans.

"Many of the large, mature trees in the area were incorporated into our design, complementing the common areas and park areas," says Hampton. "We strive to design all our developments with plenty of green spaces and well landscaped areas for the utmost in pleasant living. New bike paths are planned for the Vintage Heights area, and several popular golf courses are located in the area."

Another HDS development is Ridge Pointe, a prestigious area of one-half to three-quarter-acre lots at 27th and Pine Lake Road, near SouthPointe and Williamsburg. Both of these areas are just minutes from the SouthPointe Pavilions center, for convenient shopping, entertainment, and popular restaurants.

One of Hampton's newest developments is Savannah Pines, just south of Williamsburg Village at 40th Street and Pine Lake Road. HDS teamed up with Cameron Corporation to construct one of the finest retirement communities in the Lincoln area. Savannah Pines is modeled after vacation resorts, with all-inclusive services for carefree retirement living. Waterford, a new assisted care facility, is next door.

Along with these major Lincoln area developments, HDS has developed two apartment complexes in Omaha, and is part of a retirement center in Omaha and a smaller residential area in York, northeast.

"All of our projects include green spaces, plenty of commons areas and as many mature trees as possible," Bob Hampton says. "We are especially conscious of landscaping because it creates such a pleasing, healthy environment in which to live and work. We always include bike and walking paths where we can, and connect to the Lincoln trail systems whenever possible."

Hampton says their future plans call for more mixed-use developments, incorporating residential, commercial, and "flex" spaces for convenient living and working conditions for residents. "We plan and develop all our neighborhoods as if we were going to live and work within the area ourselves." ■

North Creek at 27th and I-80 Auto Mall. Photo by John F. Sanders

Williamsburg Village bike path and common area. Photo by John F. Sanders

One of Lincoln's most desirable apartment and townhome communities is Chateau Development at North Cotner Boulevard and Vine Streets.

Listeners to Lincoln's KFOR radio station have voted Chateau Development as "Lincoln's Best Apartment Community" for two of the last three years. Today, Chateau Development has more than 2,500 residents comprising a typical cross-section of Lincoln's population, from students to retired.

and attractive landscaping. Building design and site layout give the feel of low-density housing, even though it's an apartment and townhome community.

Chateau Development comprises several distinct areas, including the original developments of Charleston Court, Chateau LaFleur, and Chateau LaFleur Townhomes. Chateau Meadows and Adriana Court apartments were added to the area in the 1980s. Chateau Gardens, an apartment community for residents over 55 years of age, was completed in 1997.

The newer buildings were designed to perpetuate the "country living" feel of the area. Plus, all the newer units are sound-proofed and feature private entrances.

Otto Gaspar of Munich, Germany purchased the original Chateau Development in 1971. An accountant with a Ph.D. in economics, Otto had clients who wanted to invest in America, especially the Midwest. Otto came to Nebraska and, after much consideration, invested in the Chateau property. Along with his client investors, Otto invested some of his own funds in Chateau.

A few years later, his clients decided to sell out their share and Otto purchased the entire property outright. Since then, the Gaspar family has continued to develop the Chateau Development property on North Cotner, along with branching out to other Lincoln areas.

The company also owns Alena Court apartments at 72nd and Van Dorn Streets and is building 320 new units to add to the 112 units already there. This 56-acre property was originally the DuTeau Farm, which the Gaspar family acquired in the early 1980s.

Chateau Gardens senior community. Photo by John F. Sanders

The property includes 887 living units on 82 acres that, in the earlier days of Lincoln, were part of a golf course and a tree nursery. The area still has a "country feel" with spacious areas of lawn, lots of mature trees,

Alena Court Apartments.

One of Chateau Development's newest projects is the new Park One office building on South 70th Street, just across the street from Holmes Lake. This four-story building has 62,800 square feet and provides attractive office spaces for several Lincoln business operations.

Otto's son, Stefan, has been managing partner for the family business since 1991, after graduating from Duke University with an MBA. Although he once entertained ideas of becoming a jazz musician, Stefan has found the real estate business challenging and rewarding.

"Our philosophy is to develop high-quality properties, but retain ownership as an investment," Stefan says. "Rather than develop and sell, we prefer to develop and expand and improve our properties for long term appreciation."

Stefan's mother, Annelies Gaspar, travels to the U.S. several times a year and still serves as the family firm's accountant. Otto, though officially "retired," still comes to Nebraska two or three times a year to review operations and progress.

"We strive to make our properties as attractive and affordable as possible," Otto says. "Our goal is to maintain them just as if they were our own home." Stefan and his family, in fact, lived in one of the Chateau apartments for 10 years.

In keeping with the family emphasis on providing quality housing, the Gaspar family donated $35,000 to Habitat for Humanity in 1998. The gift paid for all the materials to build a new home at 2010 N. 32nd Street. The gift was the largest ever given to the Lincoln Chapter of Habitat for Humanity. Stefan spent time hammering nails for the project, along with many other volunteers.

Entry to Park One office building.

More recently, Chateau Development has pledged $50,000 support to the Cornhusker Boy Scout Council over the next five years. Stefan is now serving on the boards for Habitat for Humanity and the Lincoln Public Schools Foundation. These commitments fit well with the Gaspar family's recognition of the importance of families to the Lincoln community. ■

Park One office building. Photo by John F. Sanders

 One of Lincoln's largest homebuilders, Brester Construction's work can be found in all areas of the city, especially newer developments of mid- and upscale homes. Single family housing, however, represents only about 25 percent of the company's volume. Brester Construction is unique, in that it is the only major Lincoln contractor that does both residential and commercial construction.

Besides building single family housing in all price ranges from $120,000 to over $600,000, the Brester "label" can be found on numerous commercial

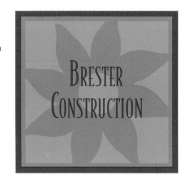

Center in Seward for the Catholic Diocese of Lincoln. This structure is now the 50,000-square-foot St. Gregory The Great Seminary.

The variety in their work stems from the previous experience of brothers Ron and Don Brester. Although both graduated with construction management degrees from the University of Nebraska-Lincoln, they went on to gain valuable experience with different construction companies, including some of the largest in the state. Their careers came together again in 1977 when they became managing partners in Crestwood Homes, responsible for construction of everything from single family homes to multi-million dollar office buildings. Ron and Don sold their interests to the other partners in 1981 and founded Brester Construction in 1982.

Today, Brester Construction is recognized as a premier Lincoln business. The company was named small business winner of the Lincoln Better Business Bureau's "Integrity Award" in 1999 and was one of 24 national finalists for the Better Business Bureau "National Torch Award" in 2000. Brester was one of 10 finalists in category III, firms with fewer than 100 employees. It was the first Lincoln contractor to be featured in the June, 1995 issue of the Nebraska/Western Iowa edition of *Builder/Architect* magazine.

Ron and Don Brester are active in local and state Home Builders Associations and the Associated General Contractors Association, and through the years both have served on numerous special project committees for the Lincoln community. All of Brester's project managers have construction management degrees from the University of Nebraska-Lincoln. ∎

Charles Senior Housing—1933 "G" Street, Lincoln, Nebraska. Photo by John F. Sanders

construction projects, including apartment complexes, retirement housing projects, office and retail buildings, school facilities, fast food restaurants, convenience stores, churches, and a golf course clubhouse. While most projects are within the Lincoln metro area, the company has completed commercial projects as far away as Kearney.

Brester Construction has established a reputation for quality remodeling and rehab work as well, including such projects as The Candy Factory, The Tool House, and the Grainger Building in Lincoln's Haymarket district. Brester was the general contractor for Waterpark, the rehabilitation of Lincoln's old power plant and water pumping station into 41 condominium units, and Hayward Place, the rehabilitation of Lincoln's oldest elementary school into condominium units. The company remodeled the former Rivendell

Malcolm Public High School, Malcolm, Nebraska. Photo by John F. Sanders

You are most likely to see ABC Electric trucks and service vehicles at major construction sites in Lincoln. But, visit many of the major commercial and public facilities in the capital city, especially at night, and you will see the results of ABC Electric's professional work.

ABC has "wired" such high profile facilities as the Lied Center for Performing Arts, Southeast and East High Schools, many buildings on the UNL campus, as well as the exterior lighting for SouthPointe Pavillions.

The company also is the primary electrical contractor for the State Capitol restoration project. According to ABC president-elect John Whitmer, that job is not only challenging but brings ABC full circle from the company's beginnings.

Whitmer's great-grandfather, Arthur Bradley Whitmer, worked on the original Nebraska State Capitol building construction in the 1920s. Shortly after that experience, A.B. and his wife, Carolyn, formed ABC Electric Company in 1932. A.B. and his son, Arthur, sold appliances in the early days to help pay the bills for the business. The business soon focused exclusively on electrical contracting, doing residential, commercial, and industrial wiring. Arthur's son, Bill Whitmer, graduated from the University of Nebraska in 1959 with a degree in electrical engineering. Bill has served as president of the company for more than 30 years and is now turning over the management responsibility to his son, John, marking the family's fourth generation to run ABC Electric Company.

ABC Electric was founded on a strong base of business ethics and service, both to customers and the community. After the devastating blizzard of October 1997, ABC Electric was one of the firms that helped get the capital city moving again. Bill Whitmer recalls that many of his servicemen put in 12- to 16-hour days restoring electric power to homes and businesses, then took emergency calls throughout the night.

Acknowledging the professionalism and integrity of ABC Electric Company, the Cornhusker Better Business Bureau presented the firm its first annual small business "Torch Award" for Marketplace Ethics in 1998. The company also has been recognized for its

neighborhood improvement projects in the Clinton/Malone area of Lincoln, where the company is headquartered.

ABC Electric continues to evolve, keeping pace with the increasing technology of today's construction industry. "Electrical service and installation has become more complex, dictating even greater emphasis on training and safety," says John Whitmer. "We are more and more involved in the fast-moving field of data communications, including cabling for Internet access and services. Our future objectives include the use of thermographic analysis as a preventive maintenance tool to reduce the incidences of power disturbances to our customers and our city." ■

Lied Center for Performing Arts.

Wolfe Electric Co. continues to expand its services to Lincoln area builders and contractors. It is still a family-managed firm, but in 1999 Wolfe Electric became a part of Integrated Electrical Services, one of the largest electrical companies in the nation. Headquartered in Houston, Texas, IES has 80 member companies located in 140 locations across the U.S. with 15,000 employees. This merit shop company had 2000 revenues of $1.7 billion!

Retirement Center in south Lincoln are Wolfe projects. And, Wolfe Electric is the electrical contractor for Lincoln's two new branch libraries.

Dick Wolfe started Wolfe Electric in 1977, working out of his home with just one employee, his brother Dave. Before that, he graduated from Lincoln High School, then attended UNL for a year. He switched to Southeast Community College where he completed the course in Electrical Technology, graduating in 1970. He spent seven years after that going through his apprenticeship and getting his journeyman's license. He passed the Master/Contractor Test in 1977 and started his own company.

Wolfe Electric today has a staff of over 70 people, operates its own excavating crew for installing outdoor lighting systems, has an electrical pre-fab shop, and offers full-service data communications installation through its Timberline Systems division.

The company contributes to the Lincoln community in several ways, including working with Associated Builders and Contractors and the Lincoln Public Schools to provide opportunities for high school students to learn a trade through the Ventures in Partnership Program. Wolfe Electric over the years has provided both labor and materials for several non-profit projects, including several Habitat for Humanity projects. ∎

Wolfe Electric was selected as the electrical contractor for Staybridge Suites. Photo by John F. Sanders

While the affiliation with IES offers national accounts and administration, as well as field help advantages, Wolfe Electric still operates as a local, independent company. It is still a family operation. Richard (Dick) Wolfe is president, brother Dave is vice president of operations, son Jason is vice president of estimating, son-in-law Doug is vice president of Timberline Systems data company, son Kevin and brother Tom are field foremen, and Ardyth, Dick's mother, is the office secretary.

"We believe our 'family culture' helps us maintain a closer working relationship with our employees and customers, and I believe this is one of the reasons we have grown to become one of Lincoln's leaders in electrical contracting," Dick says.

The company's recent project list reads like a "Who's Who" of Lincoln building jobs. The new Park One Office Building on South 70th is a Wolfe project. So is the new Allied Insurance Building in Williamsburg. Other projects include Lincoln Christian School, and the Legacy Terrace retirement complexes at 56th and Pioneers and 56th and Fremont. The huge Savannah Pines retirement complex, and the new Waterford

The new Allied Insurance building is one of the company's more recent projects. Photo by John F. Sanders

For nearly three decades, Mega Corporation of Lincoln has provided personalized commercial real estate services in the Lincoln market.

Donald W. Linscott launched Mega Corporation in 1975, with three other licensed professionals. He recognized Lincoln's need for a real estate firm that specialized in commercial and industrial real estate, focusing on sales, leasing, and property management.

As the business expanded, other professionals were added to the Mega staff. Today there are four real estate commercial specialists, two property managers, one financial executive, one real estate assistant, and one marketing individual.

Linscott says Mega Corporation of Lincoln's objective is to maximize each client's goal by providing:
- Professional advice on a property's market value;
- An effective marketing plan, including signage, brochures, and advertising;
- Availability for listing the property in the Multiple Listing Service;
- Timely communications with the client on all aspects of the property;
- Expertise in analyzing sales and lease agreements, tenant improvements, etc.

"With the Internet and electronic communications, the way we market and the ways we interact with clients has changed, but our overall objectives and core values remain the same," Linscott says. "There has been a lot of consolidation in the industry and some large companies have emerged. We think there is still room in the industry for the 'boutique' type business that can provide personal service and effectively fill niche markets."

Mega Corporation of Lincoln— Team 2001. Photo by John F. Sanders

Mega Corporation of Lincoln has continued to grow and expand by following those precepts. Today, Mega Corporation of Lincoln is one of the most recognized firms in the Lincoln area, and the familiar green and white Mega signs can be seen on many of Lincoln's most prominent business and industry sites.

Mega Corporation of Lincoln currently manages more than 290,000 square feet of office space, 151,500 square feet of retail space, and over 1,000,000 square feet of warehouse

and industrial space. Some of the company's newest developments are:
- **Upland Business Center** on NW 12th Street, with 90,000 square feet of development area that includes two existing buildings;
- **Horizon Business Center** at 14th and Pine Lake Road, with 430,000 square feet of office, warehouse, retail, and "flex" space;
- **Professional Park North** at 26th and Ticonderoga in north Lincoln, a retail and office building with over 40,000 square feet;
- **Pioneer Greens Office Park** at 84th and Pioneers Boulevard, a new project that eventually will have several buildings and more than 134,000 square feet of space.

In addition, Mega Corporation of Lincoln has recently moved its headquarters to one of the company's newest developments at 44 Corporate Place. "We continue to grow, but we will always maintain our policy of personal attention and specialized service for our clients," Linscott says. ■

Taylor Meadows Office Park—1001 South 70th Street. Photo by John F. Sanders

CHAPTER NINE

Health Care, Education & Quality of Life

With Lincoln's growth has come an increasing need for more medical facilities and patient services. BryanLGH Medical Center has expanded to meet those needs. In fact, BryanLGH has spearheaded the development of Lincoln into a major medical center for Southeast Nebraska and, through affiliations with other facilities, throughout Nebraska and northern Kansas.

As part of its mission, BryanLGH Medical Center provides comprehensive medical services at two Lincoln facilities, as well as providing the key element of a network that delivers sophisticated mobile diagnostic treatment and services to citizens throughout the region. As part of the Heartland Health Alliance, a statewide network of 32 hospitals, BryanLGH has forged strong partnerships with other hospitals, physicians, and communities to make available high quality, cost effective health care throughout much of Nebraska and the surrounding areas.

BryanLGH Medical Center has a nationally recognized heart program, and has been designated a 100 Top Hospital for cardiovascular services by Solucient for three consecutive years. BryanLGH also placed in the 100 Top Hospital ranking in 2000 for its orthopedic services and in 2001 for stroke care.

Overall, BryanLGH is known nationally for its quality of medical care and special services. It is recognized as a Medicare Renal Disease Treatment Center and a Level II Trauma Center. It has the only Medicare-approved Adult Heart Transplant program in Nebraska. BryanLGH is accredited by the Joint Commission on Accreditation for Health Care Organizations, and is a member of the Nebraska Association of Hospitals and Health Systems, the American Hospital Association, and the National Cardiovascular Network.

It began more than 90 years ago, when the Lincoln Hospital Association was incorporated in 1910. That association established Lincoln General Hospital in 1925. Meanwhile, in 1920, local ministers and laymen created a board to establish Lincoln Methodist Hospital. When William Jennings Bryan donated his

home, Fairview, and five acres to the board in 1922, the name was changed to Fairview Methodist Hospital. It became Bryan Memorial Hospital in 1925, following William Jennings Bryan's death, and opened with 47 beds in 1926. These two hospitals merged in 1997, establishing BryanLGH Medical Center.

Today, BryanLGH is a 583-bed, not-for-profit, locally owned healthcare organization with two acute-care facilities—BryanLGH East and BryanLGH West. BryanLGH also operates several outpatient clinics, including a new 4-story, outpatient facility called Pine Lake Medical Plaza, to better serve Lincoln's growing southeastern area. That location will house physician offices and expanded outpatient diagnostic and treatment services.

Major construction projects also are underway at both BryanLGH East and BryanLGH West. These projects include an expanded state-of-the-art emergency department/trauma center, total remodeling of inpatient care areas, a new mental health inpatient unit, a new building for the Independence Center (chemical dependency treatment), and new medical offices and parking facilities at BryanLGH West.

At BryanLGH East, new construction includes expanded cardiovascular facilities, adding more critical care beds and more space for new cardiac technology and support services. A new Women's Center is also being added, along with complete renovation of the obstetrics and gynecological services area to achieve greater operating efficiency and provide even higher levels of service.

With specific clinical areas located at each facility, duplication of services is eliminated and overall level of care is enhanced. The overall projects will add another 63 beds to BryanLGH capacity.

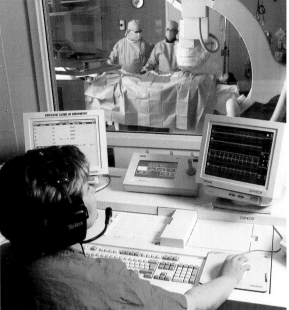

Heart Catheterization Lab.

BryanLGH Medical Center is expanding in response to the growing needs of a growing community. From 1995-2000, BryanLGH experienced a 23.7 percent increase in inpatient volumes, 22.9 percent increase in outpatient volumes, and 29 percent increase in emergency services. New medical technology advances are coming along at ever-increasing rates, and BryanLGH intends to stay on the leading edge with state-of-the-art facilities and procedures.

The combined strength of the BryanLGH facilities provides unique opportunities for acquiring both equipment and expertise for the newest developments in medical procedures. For example, Nebraska's first Gamma Knife Center is located at BryanLGH West. Developed originally in Sweden, Gamma Knife Radiosurgery is a non-invasive medical procedure that uses focused beams of radiation to treat lesions in the brain without open surgery.

Gamma Knife Radiosurgery is the treatment of choice for small and medium-sized brain lesions, which often were considered inoperable in the past. Gamma Knife and radiation oncology programs form the basis for greater levels of service in neuro-sciences and oncology.

Known for the past 30 years as the state's leading heart program, BryanLGH continues to lead the way in cardiovascular procedures. The latest treatment and technology at BryanLGH includes Ross surgical procedures, heart assist devices (mechanical hearts), heart laser surgical procedures, limited-incision and off-pump bypass surgeries, and coronary vascular brachytherapy.

The BryanLGH heart team travels more than a million miles annually, partnering with more than 40 Nebraska communities to provide a variety of diagnostic and treatment services. This includes the state's first and only mobile heart catheterization lab, mobile nuclear scanning labs, and mobile vascular services.

Nebraska Gamma Knife Center.

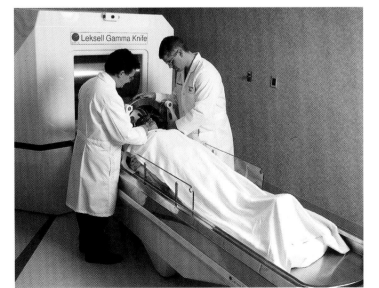

JDRF Walk to Cure Diabetes.

Medical advances, however, are only part of the story at BryanLGH Medical Center. As an organization, BryanLGH provides numerous benefits to the community and individual patients and families.

The Medical Center sponsors ongoing classes, as well as annual programs such as Heart Month activities, Kids' Health and Safety Fair, and school tours that expose both children and adults to healthy lifestyle habits and the hospital environment. The BryanLGH A'la Heart Dining Program reaches hundreds of participants each year, providing cooking demonstrations, recipes, and tips for heart healthy meals. The BryanLGH Community Health Education and Resource Center brings nationally known guests and speakers to Lincoln to focus attention on topics that affect women, children, and families.

Individually, hundreds of the 3,600 employees of BryanLGH Medical Center participate in community services and activities, including events like the March of Dimes WalkAmerica, American Heart Association Walk, Lincoln Marathon, and Junior Achievement activities, to name just a few.

Collectively, BryanLGH staff members work with many support groups, including Ex-Smokers, Pulmonary Rehab, and others. Employees participate with Lincoln Public Schools in their Ventures in Partnership program, facilitating on-site experience for Lincoln High School school-to-work students and partnering with students and faculty from Lefler Middle School and Holmes Elementary School. BryanLGH has also actively supported the Star City Holiday Parade since its inception in 1986.

Community Health Education and Resource Center.

BryanLGH established the first experimental learning program for high schoolers in the mid-1980s. The program has since served as a model for expanding experimental learning programs to other organizations. The Lefler Middle School partnership was recognized with a Pioneer Award in 1995 and special recognition in 1996 as the first program to provide mentors for middle school students.

BryanLGH further extends its overall mission with annual investments of more than $3 million in subsidized programs and services, which provide education for healthcare professionals as well as helping meet the physical, educational, and emotional needs of patients and their families.

Examples of these special programs include the School of Nurse Anesthesia, Center for Advanced Nursing Practice, Center for Bioethics, Lincoln Medical Education Foundation Family Practice Residency Program, and the Bryan School of Nursing. Throughout the year, the Medical Center conducts numerous special activities and medical services for its 55PLUS program for Lincoln's older adults.

BryanLGH Medical Center is committed to providing the most comprehensive range of healthcare services and employing the latest technology and treatments available. The BryanLGH mission statement best reflects the Medical Center's goal for the future: "The mission of BryanLGH Medical Center is to provide our community, state, and region a comprehensive continuum of patient-centered care in cooperation with other healthcare providers. We provide education to healthcare professions, promote wellness, provide quality healthcare services for those in need regardless of their ability to pay, and are sensitive to those who are culturally diverse or have disabilities." ■

I t began as a frontier hospital in 1889, when four pioneering Sisters of St. Francis of Perpetual Adoration came to Lincoln and established a hospital in a home on South Street. Local Catholic Bishop Thomas Bonacum had raised $20,000 and purchased the residence from the Buckstaff family. They were still living there when the sisters arrived, so the sisters moved into the basement and stored their provisions in the barn.

Lincoln had just 13,000 residents in those days. Typhoid, small pox, diptheria, and scarlet fever took

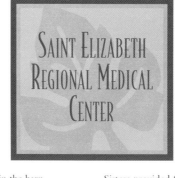

SAINT ELIZABETH REGIONAL MEDICAL CENTER

heavy tolls on citizens, especially children. By January 1, 1890, 26 patients had been treated at Saint Elizabeth. Nine were charity cases. Payment to the sisters often was in the form of chickens, vegetables, or hay.

Saint Elizabeth's nursery was opened in 1918, although several babies and young mothers had been treated in the earlier years. Sisters provided free care for mothers and babies who had no financial resources. By 1942, Saint Elizabeth was known as the baby hospital, with 677 births. Today, more than 2,200 babies are born at the hospital every year.

Saint Elizabeth Regional Medical Center is still recognized for its maternity, which include general OB, a maternal-fetal medicine program for high-risk mothers and babies, a general nursery, Lincoln's only neonatal intensive care unit, (NICU) which serves a 29 county/state region.

Saint Elizabeth today is a corporate partner with Catholic Health Initiatives, one of the nation's largest Catholic health systems. Saint Elizabeth gives that system a strong Nebraska presence. Located on South 70th Street, Saint Elizabeth Regional Medical Center has recently begun construction on a new medical office building and a new patient tower to meet the communities growing needs for medical care. Outreach services include several clinics and two stand-alone urgent care centers in Lincoln and the surrounding area. The hospital's medical staff includes 429 physicians. Other services include an Occupational Health program, Home Care services, and many specialty clinics.

Saint Elizabeth Heart team performs a variety of open heart and other cardiac procedures regularly.

In 1893, in its fifth year, Saint Elizabeth moved into this "modern" facility on 11th and South Streets.

Saint Elizabeth has a rapidly growing, leading edge cardiovascular program
that includes a full range of diagnostic,
invasive, and non-invasive heart procedures, including off-pump surgery.
The hospital has a fully equipped
Cardiopulmonary Rehab Center on site
and offers a wide range of rehabilitation
programs geared to each individual
patient's needs.

Saint Elizabeth opened the region's
first Burn Center in 1973 and is now
a multi-state referral center for burn
patients. The unit organizes and coor-
dinates teaching activities with area
firefighters and paramedics to assure the
best care possible for burn victims. The
hospital has expanded the Burn Center
to include Wound Care and is nationally
known for its outstanding research.

Saint Elizabeth offers a full spectrum
of medical services that includes adult
clinics in pulmonology, speech and
swallowing, natural family planning,
and the EMG clinic. Radiology services
include complete mammography
screening and diagnostics. Medical/
oncology services are built around an
atmosphere of caring and support for
cancer patients and families, including chemotherapy
and hospice services when needed.

*High quality care
and technology combine
with medical teamwork
to provide their
patients an unexcelled
healing environment.*

Today, Saint Elizabeth continues to emphasize
children's care. Services include pediatric specialty
clinics, cardiology, diabetes, EMG, endocrinology, G.I.,
pulmonary, oncology, neurodiagnostics, pediatric and
infant pneumograms, acute care, and home-care services.

Saint Elizabeth also contributes to the community
as a major economic factor, with more than 1,800
employee/associates. Many are active in charitable
and community service organizations, as well as their
ministry through carrying out their hospital duties.
They continue to nurture the rich traditions, values,
and original mission of the sisters of Saint Francis of
Perpetual Adoration.

As Saint Elizabeth Regional Medical Center moves
on into the new millennium, it continues to focus
on its mission to nurture the healing ministry of the
church by bringing it new life, energy, and viability in
the 21st century.

Saint Elizabeth's mission statement includes this
charge: "Fidelity to the Gospel urges us to emphasize
human dignity and social justice as we move toward
the creation of healthier communities." ■

*More than 2,200
babies a year are born
at Saint Elizabeth.*

For a community of fewer than one-quarter million people, Lincoln can be proud of its role as an outstanding regional medical center. One of the pioneer organizations that helped Lincoln achieve this reputation is the Nebraska Heart Institute.

With a vision of expanding cardiac care services to Lincoln and greater Nebraska, cardiologists Charles Wilson, MD; Sachi Mahapatra, MD; Chris Caudill, MD; Joe Gard, MD; and cardiac surgeons Steve Carveth, MD; Herb Reese, MD; and Deepak Gangahar, MD established the Nebraska Heart Institute in 1987. NHI is headquartered in Lincoln and offers cardiac services at both BryanLGH East and BryanLGH West, Saint Elizabeth Regional Medical Center, and through outstate offices at Hastings, Grand Island, and North Platte.

The concept of the Nebraska Heart Institute originated with the desire of the founding physicians to expand both their own range of services as well as those of other medical providers in the Lincoln area. Long before NHI, one of the founders, Dr. Steve Carveth, was the moving force in creating the emergency response team at Memorial Stadium for home football games. The response team set-up became a model used by other universities, and by other venues where large crowds gathered.

Also in the mid-1960s, Dr. Carveth helped organize Lincoln's Mobile Heart Team. The first two angioplasty procedures in Nebraska were done by another one of NHI's founders, Dr. Christopher Caudill, on February 18, 1981.

The Nebraska Heart Institute performs more than 1,500 open-heart procedures annually.

Today, NHI delivers leading-edge cardiac care services to much of rural Nebraska and northern Kansas through a network of 45 affiliated clinics and hospitals in smaller communities. In fact, the Nebraska Heart Institute regularly draws patients from several surrounding states, including Colorado, Oklahoma, Iowa, South Dakota, and the Kansas City area. It's because of the high level of experience and specialization within NHI's staff of 28 cardiologists and surgeons, along with a quality support staff of 210 people.

The Nebraska Heart Institute has been a proven leader in cardiac, thoracic, and vascular services since its inception in 1987. Photo by John F. Sanders

NHI is the only heart transplant center in Nebraska, performing an average of one heart, lung, or cardiac assist implant device transplant every month. The institute performs about 1,600 open-heart surgeries annually and more than 6,000 "Cath Lab" procedures at NHI's own cardiac catheterization labs and cath labs at area hospitals.

NHI physicians have pioneered the delivery of top quality cardiac care to small towns and rural communities through their network affiliation with family physicians and primary care providers in those areas. The NHI specialists make scheduled trips to the smaller towns, frequently by charter aircraft, to consult with family doctors, see cardiac patients, and provide follow-up support to post-operative patients.

For the primary care physician who provides the initial patient referral, NHI offers experienced skills to support the primary care physician's treatment program. NHI physicians often handle follow-up patient visits when requested by the referring physician. And, NHI physicians are always "on call" by telephone or electronic media. Results over the years show that cardiac patients who can be followed-up in their own local community tend to require shorter hospital stays and have less post-operative stress.

The NHI mobile cardiac catheterization laboratory, operated in association with BryanLGH, was only the fourth mobile heart facility established in the U.S. and the first one focused on serving rural areas. NHI and local hospitals provide mobile cardiac diagnostic services, including nuclear cardiology, echocardiogram (ECG),

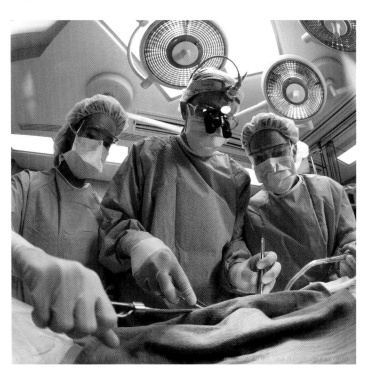

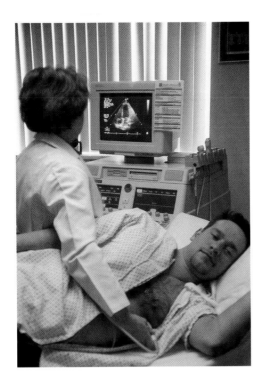

Diagnostic testing is performed from NHI's main Lincoln offices as well as more than 40 communities throughout the region. Photo by John F. Sanders

and associated vascular studies to communities such as Valentine, North Platte, and Lexington—traveling up to 300 miles from Lincoln to bring expert cardiac services to rural Nebraskans. NHI also partners with BryanLGH in a computerized ECG network, through which heart test readings can be instantly transmitted from an outlying clinic to Lincoln for heart specialist consultation.

The reputation of NHI as a leading cardiac care provider has enabled the institute to participate in numerous national studies and research programs. NHI is one of 20 sites in the U.S. participating in new

mechanical heart evaluation. NHI was one of the first cardiac centers in the country to investigate the use of laser surgery for heart disease. It was also the first facility in this region to do off-pump coronary bypass surgery (OPCAB), a procedure that causes less trauma to the patient's system. NHI now has one of the top OPCAB programs in the country. The institute is also taking an active role in studying the use of robotics for cardiac surgery.

By combining forces, the physicians who formed NHI have been able to attract even more specialized and experienced doctors to the institute staff and to Lincoln. Through their networking with other areas of medicine, such as oncology, radiology, hematology, and others, they have helped draw additional medical resources to the area. This has helped Lincoln become a major tertiary care center, benefiting the medical needs of the entire region.

Each year, the institute's skilled physician teams perform more diagnostic, interventional, and surgical procedures than any other cardiac program in Nebraska. With their outreach, they also bring the finest in cardiac care services to Nebraska residents who otherwise would have to travel long distances or who would not have access to the latest medical technology procedures.

NHI physicians established the Lincoln Heart Improvement Program in 1993, a collaborative effort with primary care physicians that offers multidisciplinary, comprehensive cardiac evaluation and treatment of congestive heart failure patients. NHI also formed the Women's Heart Program, which provides comprehensive cardiac evaluation, risk-factor assessment and corrective recommendations specifically for women's needs, as well as the Arrythmia and Syncope Clinic. ■

The Nebraska Heart Institute performs more than 6,000 cardiac catheterizations, 1,700 interventions, and 600 electrical device implants. Photo by John F. Sanders

It began in 1958 as Madonna Home, a long-term care facility for the elderly. Today, Madonna Rehabilitation Hospital is a modern 254-bed facility that serves over 3,500 patients a year.

Madonna is still located on the original 22-acre campus in south Lincoln, but the grounds today include spacious lawns, shade trees, courtyards, sculpture gardens, and walking paths, all designed for enhancing the comfort and well being of patients and staff.

![Madonna Rehabilitation Hospital logo]

MADONNA
REHABILITATION
HOSPITAL

The 24-hour care facility provides a first-of-its-kind choice—the opportunity for adults with disabilities to live in a community environment rather than a nursing home.

Madonna Rehabilitation Hospital has led the way both regionally and nationally in innovative rehabilitation programs. The hospital received the nation's first Medicare certification in 1966, when it began offering rehabilitation services. Madonna was one of the first rehabilitation facilities in the nation to collaborate with a burn trauma center for comprehensive therapy for burn patients outside of the typical hospital burn unit. Madonna's Long Term Acute Care Hospital provides a special 30-bed facility for patients with multiple medical complications and functional disabilities, at less cost than similar treatment in an acute-care hospital.

Madonna's reputation brings patients to the hospital from a wide area. Last year, Madonna Rehabilitation Hospital served 3,730 people from 286 Nebraska towns and 21 states. More than 600 physicians referred patients from 111 different hospitals.

Madonna thrives because of its unique attention to "culture." The hospital and its 930 employees operate under a "systems chart" rather than the typical organization chart. The systems chart is based on functions, processes, and tasks that cross department lines and promote flexibility and teamwork in enabling Madonna Rehabilitation Hospital to carry out its mission of service. ■

Employees of Madonna take the extra time needed to assist patients back to a healthy life. Photo by John F. Sanders

Madonna's reputation brings patients to the hospital from a wide area. Last year, Madonna Rehabilitation Hospital served 3,730 people from 286 Nebraska towns and 21 states. Photo by John F. Sanders

The hospital has undergone major expansions and renovations in the past 10 years, including a new wing with private rooms and baths. The Institute for Rehabilitation Science and Engineering at Madonna Rehabilitation Hospital includes a new gait and motion laboratory, new speech pathology laboratory, added conference spaces, and a special Telehealth installation for rehabilitation consultation with other hospitals via satellite. Twenty-four formal, applied research projects are under way at the Institute.

Unique facilities include the James E. Ryan Memorial Chapel, offering Catholic, Protestant, and ecumenical services for people with disabilities; and Independence Square, a simulated community within the hospital for "real life" therapy sessions.

Completed in 2000, Madonna's new Assisted Living House is the only one of its kind in the United States designed to serve persons who use ventilators. It is designed for adults 19-59 with severe disabilities.

"Making a difference, touching lives—one person at a time." This statement captures the essence of what Tabitha Health Care Services is all about. For more than 115 years, Tabitha has embraced a legacy of caring and a mission of developing services to meet unmet social, health care, and spiritual needs in local communities. Affiliated with the Evangelical Lutheran Church in America, Tabitha's motto reflects its Christian roots: "Tabitha cares because Christ cares."

Tabitha's founder would be delighted today at the operation he started. Rev. Heinrich Heiner put a $25 down payment on a 10-acre tract at 48th and Randolph Streets in 1886, and moved a group of homeless and orphaned children into an old, dilapidated cowboy bunkhouse on the property. Homeless elders soon moved in. Heiner called the organization "Tabitha" after his own daughter, who had died in infancy. She was named after a woman in the Book of Acts who was known for "deeds of kindness and charity."

Today, Tabitha Nursing & Rehabilitation Center has replaced the bunkhouse and is known as a premiere facility for comprehensive rehabilitation, Alzheimer's/dementia services, hospice, and long-term care. Located on the same campus, Tabitha Corporate Headquarters directs the most complete continuum of pre- and post-hospital services offered in 32 Nebraska counties, with regional corporate offices in York and Nebraska City and satellite offices in nine more locations across the state.

TABITHA HEALTH CARE SERVICES

Tabitha is a leader in the home care industry and was the first Nebraska organization—one of just six in the entire nation—to provide home health care. Tabitha's Home Health Care program became Medicare certified in 1966, and later expanded to provide private duty, extended hour home care through Home Care Specialties of Tabitha. Tabitha averages over 50,000 home health visits every year.

Tabitha initiated Nebraska's first "Meals on Wheels" program in 1967. Now, close to 350 homebound people receive a hot noon meal, seven days a week, from Tabitha's kitchens.

Hospice of Tabitha was introduced in 1979—again the first hospice program in this area and the longest serving. Tabitha assists family members to care for loved ones with a terminal illness at home, and offers a specialized hospice unit with 11 private rooms at Tabitha Nursing & Rehabilitation Center.

Another first was the opening in 1999 of the Kimmel Solarium at Tabitha, a 5,100-square-foot facility for individuals with Alzheimer's and other forms of dementia. The Kimmel Solarium is a state-of-the-art all-weather activity center offering therapeutic recreation programs and adult day services.

Tabitha has been a leader in affordable housing for seniors since the early '70s. Tabitha Housing Corporation oversees 275 living units with over 300 tenants, including 21 units in Fairbury where Tabitha's Old Trail Restaurant and Doozy's franchise are also located.

Tabitha has returned to its roots by opening an Intergenerational Day Care Center for children and adults. Tabitha also has partnered with Immanuel Retirement Communities to co-sponsor "The Landing," a new retirement and assisted living community scheduled for completion in late 2001 in Williamsburg Village. ■

Tabitha staff truly make a difference in the lives of many Nebraskans. Photo by John F. Sanders

Tabitha Nursing & Rehabilitation Center is located at 48th and Randolph Streets. Photo by John F. Sanders

When five Lincoln families got together in 1951 to form the first Christian school in Lincoln, they had two primary purposes: Provide their children an excellent education and present it in the light of God's Word.

Now, as Lincoln Christian School celebrates its 50th anniversary, those objectives are being met in far-reaching ways that the founders could hardly have imagined. LCS today has a diverse student body of more than 650 students in grades K-12. Students represent 62 different churches and more than 400 Lincoln-area families.

LINCOLN CHRISTIAN SCHOOL

home honors nearly every time. The LCS drama department consistently ranks among the top three in the Centennial Conference.

LCS also supports strong athletic programs as a member of the Nebraska School Activities Association, and competes in the C-1 class against other area schools. LCS volleyball and basketball teams consistently achieve statewide recognition. The LCS football program continues to grow and improve its winning record. LCS students have won numerous awards in track, cross-country, wrestling, and tennis.

The original mission of Lincoln Christian School—to teach the truth by studying God's world in the light of God's Word—continues to provide the guiding principles for LCS programs, activities, and personnel. Daily Bible classes and weekly chapel services are a regular part of the schedule. Spiritual emphasis weeks are conducted for all grade levels, and students have the opportunity to participate in mission trips and local community outreach programs.

The goal is to help students achieve sound spiritual, moral, educational, and social development to the utmost of their abilities, in a supportive, encouraging environment in which each student can build his relationship with God through faith in Jesus Christ. ■

Lincoln Christian School– learning about God's world in the light of God's Word. Photo by John F. Sanders

Lincoln Christian is a parent-owned school, situated on a 35-acre campus at 84th and Old Cheney. Families automatically become members of the LCS Association when their children are enrolled. Tuition fees and tax-deductible contributions fund the school. The LCS Foundation provides additional capital and endowment funding through tax deductible gifts and planned estate gifts. Using the Lincoln Public Schools average of $6,200 cost per student per year, LCS actually saves local taxpayers over $4 million per year.

While LCS offers parents an alternative school choice, the institution works closely with the Nebraska Department of Education and LPS to ensure that LCS students receive the best education possible. Lincoln Christian received state accreditation in 2001. LCS teachers are all certified and many have multiple academic degrees. All are committed to serving Christ and the school community.

LCS supports an active speech, music, and drama education program for both elementary and secondary students. The music curriculum includes basic music education, along with opportunities to participate in choral and instrumental activities. LCS students and music groups take part in several musical events and competitions throughout the school year and bring

Lincoln Christian School students test well above the national and state average in yearly academic testing. Photo by John F. Sanders

The Lied Center is based in Lincoln, but it plays a major role in bringing performing arts to the entire state. "Our goal," says Executive Director Charles Henry Bethea, "is to make the performing arts accessible to as many citizens as possible."

The Lied Center hosts a wide-ranging variety of performers and productions every season. A typical schedule includes some 40 different events and over 100,000 tickets sold each year.

But the Lied gets much more use. Facilities are rented or loaned to local community groups and UNL organizations for as many as 80 additional activities per year. When all these special events are included with the Lied Center's own performances, upwards of 250,000 persons pass through its doors annually.

The Lied Center also conducts a major outreach program each year, beyond the center's own stages. At least half the artists and groups that perform at the Lied also conduct special performances, workshops, or training sessions for local schools, the University of Nebraska, Lincoln area senior centers, even local correctional facilities.

Lied staff members network with other Nebraska communities, too, and many artists and groups put on their shows in greater Nebraska communities before or after appearing at the Lied Center. Plus, visiting artists and Lied staff frequently assist local and area organizations stage performances in their own venues.

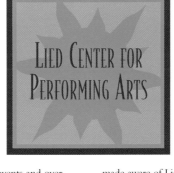

LIED CENTER FOR PERFORMING ARTS

The Lied Center for Performing Arts main hall seats over 2,200 guests. Photo by John F. Sanders

"Friends of Lied" is a statewide organization of nearly 1,000 contributing members who not only support Lied Center activities, but actively assist with fund-raising programs to extend the Lied outreach across Nebraska. Friends of Lied members often organize bus trips to see major Lied performances, as well as working to ensure that communities across the state are made aware of Lied activities and services.

The Lied Center is self-sustaining, operating with revenue from ticket sales, rental of facilities, donations,

and endowment funds. The center receives no subsidies from the University of Nebraska or the state of Nebraska. Lied operates with a paid staff of about 35 people, including its own maintenance staff, plus volunteer help for major performances and events and occasionally for administrative tasks.

The Lied Center opened February 9, 1990, with the Opera/Omaha performance of "Madama Butterfly." It culminated a major organization and fund-raising effort that began in 1983 with retired UNL president D. B. "Woody" Varner. He secured a $10 million commitment from the Lied Trust towards the construction of a performing arts center as a lasting memorial to Omaha native Ernest Lied and his parents, E. M. and Ida K. Lied.

After raising another $10 million from private and state funds, the project got underway and was completed in late 1989. Additional endowment funds provide continuing support for Lied Center operations and funding support for the many quality programs brought to the center each year. ■

The Lied Center for Performing Arts is located on the University of Nebraska-Lincoln campus. The Center serves students and residents of the entire region by bringing the world's finest art and entertainment to its stage. Photo by John F. Sanders

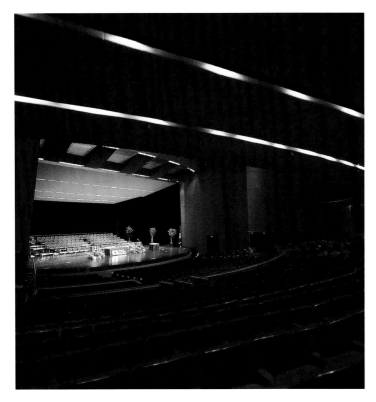

Enterprise Index

M.E. Group
2820 North 48th Street, #200
Lincoln, Nebraska 68504
Phone: 402-464-3833
Fax: 402-464-3919
E-mail: meg@megroup.com
www.megroup.com
Page 117

Madonna Rehabilitation Hospital
5401 South Street
Lincoln, Nebraska 68506
Phone: 402-489-7102
Fax: 402-483-9460
E-mail: feedback@madonna.org
www.madonna.org
Page 150

Mega Corporation of Lincoln
300 North 44th Street, Suite 100
Lincoln, Nebraska 68503
Phone: 402-467-1234
Fax: 402-467-3456
E-mail: donl@megalnk.com
www.megalnk.com
Page 139

Molex
700 Kingbird Road
Lincoln, Nebraska 68521
Phone: 402-475-1700, extension 8215
Fax: 402-475-3426
E-mail: geden@molex.com
www.molex.com
Page 100

NEBCO, Inc.
1815 Y Street
Lincoln, Nebraska 68508
Phone: 402-434-1212
Fax: 402-434-1799
Pages 130-131

Nebraska Heart Institute
1500 South 48th Street, Suite 800
Lincoln, Nebraska 68506
Phone: 402-489-6555
Fax: 402-483-8708
E-mail: info@neheart.com
www.nebraskaheart.com
Pages 148-149

Novartis Consumer Health, Inc.
10401 Highway 6
Lincoln, Nebraska 68501
Phone: 402-464-6311
Fax: 402-467-8833
www.novartis.com
Pages 98-99

Pfizer
601 West Cornhusker Highway
Lincoln, Nebraska 68521-3596
Phone: 402-475-4541
Fax: 402-441-2416
Pages 94-95

Saint Elizabeth Regional Medical Center
555 South 70th Street
Lincoln, Nebraska 68510-2494
Phone: 402-486-7445
Fax: 402-486-8959
www.saintelizabethonline.com
Pages 146-147

Security Financial Life
PO Box 82248
4000 Pine Lake Road
Lincoln, Nebraska 68501
Phone: 402-434-9500
   402-434-9585 (Lois Akin direct)
Fax: 402-434-9695
E-mail: lakin@secmut.com
www.securityfinanciallife.com
Page 113

Staybridge Suites
2701 Fletcher Avenue
Lincoln, Nebraska 68504
Phone: 402-438-7829
Fax: 402-438-7865
E-mail: sherri@sbs-lincoln.com
www.sbs-lincoln.com
Page 110

Tabitha Health Care Services
4720 Randolph Street
Lincoln, Nebraska 68510
Phone: 402-486-8559
Fax: 402-486-8528
E-mail: publicaf@tabitha.org
www.tabitha.org
Page 151

Talent+
5220 South 16th Street, Suite 1
Lincoln, Nebraska 68512
Phone: 402-489-2000
Fax: 402-489-4156
E-mail: smaxwell@talentplus.com
www.talentplus.com
Page 118

UNICO Group, Inc.
4435 O Street
Lincoln, Nebraska 68510
Phone: 402-434-7200
Fax: 402-434-7272
E-mail: sbair@unicogroup.com
www.unicogroup.com
Page 115

Union Bank
4732 Calvert Street
Lincoln, Nebraska 68506
Phone: 402-323-1828
www.ubt.com
Page 116

Uniservice, Inc.
3300 North 41st Street
Lincoln, Nebraska 68504
Phone: 402-464-6326
Fax: 402-464-9506
E-mail: office@uniserviceinc.com
www.uniserviceinc.com
Page 102

Wells Fargo Bank
1248 O Street
Lincoln, Nebraska 68508
Phone: 402-434-4321
www.wellsfargo.com
Pages 106-107

Wolfe Electric Company, Inc.
7121 Amanda Road
Lincoln, Nebraska 68507
Phone: 402-464-4333
Fax: 402-464-4366
E-mail: dick@wolfeelectric.com
Page 138

Woods Bros. Realty
4645 Normal Boulevard
Lincoln, Nebraska 68506
Phone: 402-434-3500
Fax: 402-434-8191
E-mail: relocation@woodsbros.com
www.woodsbrosrealty.com
Pages 124-125

Acknowledgements

In recognition of their invaluable cooperation, advice, and insight to ensure the accurate and comprehensive development of *Seasons of Lincoln*, Community Communications, Inc., wishes to sincerely thank the following members of the *Seasons of Lincoln* Honorary Advisory Committee:

Craig Andresen, KFRX FM 102.7

Rodney Bates, KUON–TV

Kathy Campbell, County Commission

David Dwinell, KLKN–TV 8

John Chapo, Folsom Children's Zoo and Botanical Gardens

Andrew Cheesman, Lincoln Lighting

Deane Finnegan, Leadership Lincoln

Diane Gonzolas, Citizen Information Center

Dennis Haun, Strategic Air Command Museum

Dwain Hebda, *Lincoln Business Journal*

Mike Johanns, Governor

Gary Johnson, WOWT–TV 6

James Locklear, Nebraska Statewide Arboretum

Sara McLoughlin, Junior League

James Morgan, Parks and Recreation Department

Roger Reynolds, Home Builders Association of Lincoln

Philip Schoo, Lincoln Public Schools

Suzi Shugert, Lincoln Arts Council

Dr. David Smith, Union College

Dr. Dennis Smith, University of Nebraska

Earl Visser, Optimist Club

Jeanie Watson, Nebraska Wesleyan University

Don Wesley, Mayor

John Wood, Lincoln Airport Authority

Pace Woods, Lincoln Board of Realtors

Index